# Fifty Sermon Outlines on the Way of Salvation

Jeff D. Brown

A Division of Baker Book House Co
Grand Rapids, Michigan 49516

© 1959 by Baker Book House Company

Published by Baker Books
a division of Baker Book House Company
P.O. Box 6287, Grand Rapids, MI 49516-6287

New paperback edition published 2001

Printed in the United States of America

All rights reserved. No part of this publication may be reproduced, stored in a retrieval system, or transmitted in any form or by any means—for example, electronic, photocopy, recording—without the prior written permission of the publisher. The only exception is brief quotations in printed reviews.

ISBN 0-8010-9128-4

For current information about all releases from Baker Book House, visit our web site:
http://www.bakerbooks.com

# CONTENTS

3

# CHRIST IS CALLING
## JOHN 11:20-29

Introduction.

1. Scripture story . . .
2. Text, v. 28—"The Master is come and calleth for you" . . .
3. When Christ calls, it is a personal call . . .

## I. HE CALLS MEN TO HIMSELF . . .

1. This is a call to peace . . .
2. To a guiltless conscience . . .
3. To a full pardon from sin . . .
4. To a new life in Christ . . .

## II. HE CALLS MEN IN THE DARK HOURS . . .

1. V. 15 . . .
2. Martha said, "If thou hadst been . . . " — Jesus said in effect: "I'm glad I was not" . . .
    (a) That ye may believe . . .
    (b) That His power might be revealed and thereby others would believe . . .
    (c) That there be no mistake about His power . . .
3. Trouble is often the only door through which Jesus can get to the heart . . .

## III. HE CALLS MEN IN MANY WAYS . . .

1. Through preaching of the Word—Romans 10:13-17 . . .
2. Through providence . . .
3. Through tragedy, death, sickness, etc. . . .
4. Always through the Holy Spirit—John 16:7-13 . . .

## IV. HE IS CALLING YOU . . .

1. To confession of sin—I John 3:9 . . .
2. To repentance of sin—Acts 17:30 . . .
3. To a new birth—John 3:3-6 . . .
4. To a holy life—Romans 12:1 . . .
5. He is calling you to eternal life in Heaven—John 14:2-3 . . .
    (a) A place of many mansions . . .
    (b) A place prepared for God's people . . .

Conclusion.

1. That He might save your soul . . .
2. That He might make your life useful for God . . .
3. That you might dwell with Him eternally . . .
    "Where I am ye may be also . . . "

WILL YOU ANSWER HIS CALL???

# GOD'S WAY TO GOD'S HEAVEN
## ISA. 1:18-20; I JOHN 1:7-9

Introduction.    God's way to Heaven is God's remedy for sin—Men are constantly seeking remedies for bodily infirmities, and when they find them they gladly recommend them to others—Man has no remedy for sin, only God—Man cannot prepare a way to Heaven, only God—Before a man will seek a remedy for his sin, his infirmity must become a reality—Let's note:

I.  REALITY OF SIN
   1. I Kings 8:46 . . .
   2. Isa. 64:6 . . .
   3. Rom. 3:10-12 . . .
   4. Gal. 3:22 . . .

II.  REASONS FOR SIN
   1. By one man's transgressions—Rom. 5:12 . . .
   2. Born in sin—Ps. 51:5 . . .
   3. Ps. 58:3 . . .
   4. Eph. 2:3 . . .

III.  RESULTS OF SIN
   1. Mind and conscience defiled—Titus 1:15 . . .
   2. Thoughts of the heart are evil—Mark 7:21 . . .
   3. Heart deceitful and desperately wicked—Jer. 17:9 . . .
   4. Flesh corrupt—Rom. 7:18 . . .
   5. John 8:21 . . .
   6. Rom. 6:23 . . .

IV.  REMEDY FOR SIN
   1. Reformation is not a cure—Jer. 13.23 . . .
   2. Religion will not suffice—Luke 18:11, 12; Phil. 3:4-9; Rom. 10:1-3 . . .
   3. Repentance is necessary—Luke 13:3; Acts 17:30 . . .
   4. Reconciliation must be received—I Cor. 5:18-20 . . .
   5. Redemption only through the blood of Christ—I Peter 1:18, 19 . . .
   6. Regeneration must be experienced—John 3:7; I Peter 1:23 . . .

V.  RETURN TO GOD AND RECEIVE HIS REMEDY
   1. Take words of confession and turn to the Lord—I John 1:9 . . .
   2. Receive Christ—God's only remedy—John 1:12; Acts 4:12 . . .
   3. God will not force us to take His remedy . . .
      (a) He has diagnosed your case and prescribed the remedy . . .
      (b) You must apply the prescription . . .

Conclusion.    The diagnosis is sin—The prescription is the blood of Christ . . .

WILL YOU APPLY??

6

# NEW YEAR'S RESOLUTIONS
## ISA. 19:20, 21

Introduction. In this passage, Isaiah speaks of the time when Egypt will know the Lord, and worship Him—Not only would they worship the Lord, they would make a vow to Him and keep it . . . (1) Note the reason for their making and keep this vow—verse 20; (2) Every Christian is a recipient of God's grace and mercy; therefore, ought to make vows to God, and keep them . . .

Here are some timely vows (resolutions) . . .

I.  I WILL ENDEAVOR TO BETTER UNDERSTAND THREE THINGS ABOUT THE BIBLE
   1. I will accept it as the inspired Word of God . . . II Tim. 3:16.
   2. I will accept it as my light and guide . . . Ps. 119:105.
   3. I shall keep in mind the fact that one day I will be judged by the Gospel . . . Rom. 2:16; I Cor. 3:13-15.

II.  I SHALL ENDEAVOR TO REMEMBER THREE THINGS ABOUT THE CHURCH
   1. It was purchased with the precious blood of Christ, and thus I will respect it . . . Eph. 5.25; Acts 20:28.
   2. The church is a divine institution and thus will I honor it . . . Matt. 16:18.
      (a) Jesus instituted the church . . .
      (b) He protects the church . . .
      (c) He is the head of the church . . .
   3. It is my duty to be loyal to the church . . .
      (a) Attend regularly—Heb. 10:25 . . .
      (b) Keep my membership in good standing . . .

III.  THREE THINGS THAT I VOW TO KEEP IN MIND CONCERNING CHRIST AND MY RELATIONSHIP WITH HIM
   1. Through Christ only is there salvation . . . Acts 4:12; John 14:6.
   2. Christ was sinless and therefore my example . . . I Peter 2:21, 22.
   3. I am not my own but belong to Christ . . . I Cor 6:19, 20.

Conclusion. These resolutions will greatly enrich your life.

WILL YOU ACCEPT THE CHALLENGE TO MAKE AND KEEP THESE VOWS?

7

# THE INVINCIBLE WORD
## JER. 36:1-4, 20-23, 27, 28

Introduction.
1. Men of all ages have attempted to destroy or make void the Word of God . . .
2. Here in this passage we find the picture of various ways men have tried to destroy the Word of God—only to find it invincible . . .

I. THE ATTEMPT IS MADE WITH FIRE
1. The King Jehoiakim burned the Scriptures . . .
2. Russia, likewise, gathered the Bibles and burned them . . .
3. Hitler, in his greed and power, burned the Bibles, and declared he would write his own . . .

II. THE ATTEMPT IS MADE BY CUTTING OUT PORTIONS—Verse 23
1. Many individuals and religious denominations are following the same procedures today . . .
   (a) No music—Cut out the psalms . . .
   (b) Depend on salvation by works—Cut out the Gospels, Romans, Hebrews, Ephesians, and others . . . such as Eph. 2:5, 8 and Rom. 3:24, 28
   (c) Teach salvation by baptism or church membership—Cut out such passages as:
       (1) *"Believe* on the Lord Jesus Christ . . . "
       (2) "The *gift* of God is eternal life . . . "
       (3) "Looking unto Jesus, the *Author* and *Finisher* of our faith . . . "
       (4) "No man cometh unto the Father but by me . . . "
       (5) "The blood of Jesus Christ, the Son, cleanseth us from all sin" . . .
       (6) "Ye must be *born again"* . . .
   (d) Deny that all are born in sin—Cut out such verses as Rom. 3:23; Ps. 51:5; I John 1:8
   (e) Compromise with sin—Cut out the epistles of Paul, Acts, the teachings of Jesus . . .
2. No stopping until all is destroyed . . .

III. THE ATTEMPT IS MADE BY MOCKERY
Ungodly men mock the Word of God and say, "If the Bible is authentic why does God allow thus and so?" . . . The Bible answers, "Whom the Lord loveth, he chasteneth" . . .

IV. THE INVINCIBLE WORD ALWAYS RETURNS WITH A SHARP WARNING TO THOSE WHO TRY TO DESTROY IT—Verses 21, 28
The Russian *people* have called for Bibles . . . Germany . . . Japan

Conclusion. The Word of God (the Bible) is complete, authentic, and invincible—"All scripture is given by inspiration of God . . . "
1. To destroy the Word is to destroy your own soul . . .
2. We must accept it *all*—Rev. 22:19 . . .
3. *Christ* and *Christ alone* must be received for salvation—all else is secondary and follows as obedience and Christian service.

WILL YOU RECEIVE CHRIST NOW?

# THIS IS THE ANSWER
## PS. 8:4a; MATT. 27:19-23

Introduction. There are many questions that come in every day life. As we raise the questions and try to answer them, we trust that we shall help you make a definite decision concerning life's most vital question, "What shall I do with Jesus, which is called Christ?"

I. WHAT AM I? . . .
1. Some philosophers and students of humanity have said that man is a God . . .
2. Others have believed that man is nothing . . . This is the answer:
   a. One thing we justly know, "Man is not God" . . .
      (1) He is neither righteous nor holy . . .
      (2) There is no sin nor crime that man has not committed . . .
   b. Another thing we know, "Man is more than nothing" . . .
      (1) He has climbed the heights, crossed the oceans . . .
      (2) Conquered barriers of life . . .
      (3) Attained intellectual knowledge . . .
      (4) Discovered and utilized natural resources . . .
      (5) Wherever one may look, we can see plainly that man is more than nothing—more than the animals . . .
   c. Man is created in divine image—he can never find his identity except by identifying himself in God . . .

II. WHY AM I HERE? . . .
1. To enjoy myself? . . .
   To this group, the world consists of a joke—life is a grand party . . .
2. To express myself? . . .
   Men ought to express their convictions—is this the main purpose of our being here? . . .
3. To find myself? . . . HERE IS THE ANSWER:
   Man created in the image of God for the express purpose of glorifying God . . .
   This can only be done by turning to God and following His will and way . . .

III. WHERE AM I GOING FROM HERE? . . .
1. Some say that death ends it all . . .
2. THIS IS THE ANSWER: . . . Whatever expression is used to designate the eternal destiny of the soul—there are but two destinies—HEAVEN and HELL . . . Scripture teaches it . . . The sixth sense of another world into which we will enter has marked the lives of every tribe and race of man . . .

Who are YOU? Why are YOU here? Where are YOU going?

# THE GREATNESS OF GOD
## PS. 104:31-35

Introduction. As one meditates upon this Psalm, it sings of the greatness of God and of the heritage of man . . .

I. HIS GLORY—verses 1, 2, 31

1. Ps. 19:1 . . . He is honored in that the heavens, the elements, depict His majesty . . .
2. He is honored by the beasts of the field, the birds of the air—they obey His laws . . .
3. Man, given the power of choice, may disobey God, may reject His love, may turn a deaf ear to His call—but in the end MUST give glory to God and acknowledge that Jesus is Christ . . . Unfortunately, this does not bring salvation (Phil. 2:11) . . .

II HIS POWER—verses 3-9

1. The winds are His messengers, the fire is His servant, the clouds are His chariot, the waters flee at His command . . .
2. His power created and controls the universe . . .
3. In His power He gives life, protects life, and preserves life . . . both physical and spiritual, and heals our afflictions . . .
4. Through His power we shall become victors over death, hell, and the grave . . .

III. HIS GRACE—Here we see the goodness of God in verses 10-25

1. God supplies water and nourishment for man and beast . . .
2. Shelter and protection for the weak . . . Think of small animals, birds —they are so colored as to hide in the foliage . . .
3. He has provided what we call natural resources that we might have what we need when we need it . . . As man makes progress God uncovers the elements to further this progress . .

IV. THE HERITAGE OF MAN

1. If God provides so well for the birds and the beasts, how much more will He provide for man . . .
2. Man, if he will accept it, may have peace within that cannot be explained . . .
3. He may have assurance of the presence and power of God in his life . . . (a) To guide his every move . . . (b) To give strength for every task . . . (c) To provide protection from every evil . . .
4. He may have happiness and joy that can come from no other source . . .
5. He may have a home in heaven where Christ Jesus shall be the constant companion . . .

Conclusion. All this hinges upon one thing—It comes through Jesus Christ . . . God offers the gift, will you receive it??

ACCEPT THIS GIFT AND YOU TOO WILL SING PSALMS—104:34

# PREPARATION FOR THE FUTURE
## AMOS 4:12

Introduction.

Definition of "prepare"—Webster says, "To make ready for, to arrange" . . .
1. Nations prepare for war—for peace, etc. . . .
2. Communities prepare for elections, social events, special occasions . . .
3. Business men prepare for sales, inventory, etc. . . .
4. Individuals prepare for holidays, vacations, trips, etc. . . .

These are all temporal—we are thinking of the spiritual preparation for the life to come. Let's look again at the Word of God . . .
1. Amos 4:12 (read) . . .
2. II Kings 20:1 . . .
3. Matt. 24:44 . . .

The future is inevitable—let's look at the preparation for it . . .

I. HELL HAS BEEN PREPARED
1. Matt. 25:41 . . .
2. Isa. 14:9 . . .

II. SATAN HAS PREPARED A TRAP
1. A trap to ensnare you . . . By deception . . .
2. This trap may seem quite innocent . . .
   (a) Such as the social practices of many . . .
   (b) The social drinker, dancing, etc. . . .
3. Enticements to keep you from the Lord's house and service . . .
   (a) Too busy with the temporal . . .
   (b) Petty grievances within the membership . . .
4. Using moral, even religious—but lost men to influence people . . .
5. In short, the Devil has set a trap to send men to hell . . .

III. GOD HAS PREPARED
1. Zeph. 1:7 . . .
2. Matt. 25:34 . . .
3. John 14:1-6 . . .
4. I. Cor. 2:9 . . .
5. God has prepared salvation through Christ Jesus that will suffice in this life and the life to come . . .
6. God has prepared sufficient power and leadership in the person of the Holy Spirit . . .
   (a) Power, not only to save, but to keep . . .
   (b) Leadership to guide every detail of life . . .
7. A place for us when the life is done . . .
8. A crown for the faithful . . .

IV. WE MUST PREPARE
1. Amos 4:12 . . .
2. By accepting and trusting Jesus . . .
3. This involves repentance, faith, confession . . .

Conclusion. The Devil has prepared for the unprepared. Jesus has prepared for the prepared.

ARE YOU PREPARED OR UNPREPARED??

# THE SECRET OF REVIVAL
## HAB. 3:2

Introduction. Two verses—Ps. 138:7 and Ps. 51:12—Text, Hab. 3:2. These verses are prayers for restoration—the revival of the individual heart—RE-VIVAL MUST BEGIN WITH INDIVIVDUALS. All great revivals involved complete stewardship—true Christianity is GIVING as well as getting, the giving of both self and substance has accompanied all great revivals.

1. At pentecost . . . (a) The people gave themselves to prayer . . . (b) To service . . . (c) To complete consecration . . . (d) To financial stewardship . . .

2. In Martin Luther's day, there was a revival we call the Reformation . . . (a) Luther gave himself completely to proclaiming the Bible in truth and purity . . . (b) The cost was great—the rewards greater . . .

3. In England, recently, in the Billy Graham campaign . . .

4. Harvests are not gathered without first a sowing . . .

The Secret of Revival Then Is:

I. GOD'S PEOPLE GIVING THEMSELVES—II Chron. 7:14
1. Completely consecrated—"Humble themselves" . . .
2. In prayer—"And pray" . . .
3. In witnessing . . .
4. In unselfishness . . .

II. GOD'S PEOPLE, CONSECRATED AND COMPASSIONATE, BRINGING LOST PEOPLE INTO THE SERVICES—Luke 14:23
1. There must be a deep interest . . .
2. We must recognize sin in its true light . . .
3. Must turn from the sin in its true light in our own lives . . .
4. Must realize the lostness of the unsaved . . .
5. We must go where they are and use our influence to bring them to Christ . . .

III. GOD GIVING THE INCREASE—I Cor. 3:6 and Ps. 127:1
1. God will give the increase when we give ourselves to the task . . .
2. When we surrender ourselves to Him, ready and willing to be used . . .
3. We must plant the seed, water, and cultivate . . .
4. Salvation is of the Lord . . .
   We are witnesses of His power . . .

Conclusion. Here is the secret of revival:
1. Giving ourselves to service . . .
2. Bringing people to Christ and the services . . .
3. God giving the increase . . .

THE FIRST STEP—GIVE YOURSELF.

## REVIVALS — WHEN NEEDED AND HOW PRODUCED
### HAB. 3:2

Introduction. As we contemplate a series of evangelistic services, we might ask, "Do we need a revival?" . . . "How can we have a real revival" . . . Let's turn to the Scriptures and find our answers.

In Rev. 1:12-16, we find the Son of Man walking among the churches as the "great head" . . .

In chapters 2 and 3, it tells us that as He walks among the churches He looks upon the work of His own hands, and too often finds it drooping, declining, dying . . . He utters His rebuke, "I know thy works—be watchful, and strengthen the things that remain, which are ready to die" . . . (1) Of Ephesus he said, "Thou has lost thy first love" . . . (2) Of Smyrna, Hypocrisy . . . (3) Of Pergamos, Idolatry . . . (4) Of Thyatira, Spiritual adultery . . . (5) Of Sardis, Complacency—"A name that thou livest, and art dead" . . . (6) Of Laodiceans, Lukewarm—another form of complacency . . . All these thought they did not need the Lord—"Thou sayest, I am rich—and have need of nothing" . . .

In each case, the Lord calls for repentance—an awakening and turning to God . . .

I. WHEN REVIVALS ARE NEEDED
1. When iniquity abounds . . . Isa. 59:2 . . .
2. When there is want of power upon the Word—no results from preaching . . .
3. When the presence of Christ in the soul is not duly prized . . . When other things are more important . . .
4. When the principles and conduct of Christians are not distinctly separate from the world . . . II Chron. 19:2 . . .

II. HOW IS A REVIVAL PRODUCED?
1. By exciting the people to pray . . .
   (a) Every great campaign of God's people has been preceded by prayer . . .
   (b) Acts 1:14—prayer before Pentecost . . .
   (c) II Chron. 7:14 . . .
2. By a manifestation of the Holy Spirit in the lives of Christians . . . Think again of Pentecost—Acts 2:41-47 . . .
3. By a steadfast adherence to the Word of God . . .
   (a) Acts 2:42—"They continued steadfastly . . . " . . .
   (b) By being examples of our teachings . . .
4. By a distinct separation of Christians from principles and practices of the ungodly . . .
   "Come ye from among them and be ye separate" . . .
When we prepare hearts in prayer and our lives by Christian living, God will send a revival . . .
5. By pouring out a spirit of love and unity upon the church . . . At Pentecost they were concerned about the needs of others . . .
6. By restoring those who have erred in doctrine and practice . . . By restoring the joy of salvation . . .
7. By saving the lost and adding them to the church—Acts 2:47 . . .

Conclusion. The need of revival is evident—the Lord is ready.
ARE YOU READY?

# THE BIBLE, THE LIVING WORD OF GOD
## MATT. 4:4

Introduction. There may be questions about the Bible . . . 1. The authority for the writings . . . 2. How the Scriptures were inspired . . . 3. Why not accept valuable historical records as the Word of God? . . . We should attempt to answer these, and other questions, as we think of the AUTHORITY, PURPOSE, AND POWER of the Bible . . .

I. AUTHORITY
    1. Inspired of God—II Tim. 3:16, 17
    2. Proofs of the inspiration and authority . . .
        (a) No portion has ever been refuted . . .
        (b) Unity—66 books written over a period of 1,000 years by many writers—yet, no conflict in record or message . . .
        (c) Preservation—many attempts to destroy, yet, intact . . .
        (d) Testimony of science . . .
        (e) Testimony of acceptance . . .
        (f) Testimony of Jesus—John 5:29 . . .
    3. The Bible is the supreme and final authority . . .
        (a) Some groups place the authority altogether in the church . . .
        (b) Others contend that each individual has authority to interpret for himself . . .
        (c) We must accept the complete and final authority of the Scriptures . . . Rev. 22:18, 19 . . .
    4. The Bible is sufficient . . .
        (a) To give us a clear and complete knowledge of God . . .
        (b) To teach us how to live a Christ-like life . . .
        (c) To teach what our relations to our fellowman should be . . .
        (d) Sufficient in life and death . . .

II. PURPOSE
    1. To reveal the will of God to man . . . Wills not the death of any . . .
    2. To reveal the wrath of God—Rom. 1:18 . . .
    3. Conviction—to convict men of sin in their lives . . .
    4. Correction in righteousness . . .
    5. Lead us to Christ . . . John 20:30, 31 . . . Gal. 3:24 . . .

III. POWER
    1. Convinces man of his need of salvation . . .
    2. Condemns the sinful nature of man . . .
    3. Separates . . . (a) In life . . . (b) In death . . .
    4. Binds in Christian love and fellowship . . .
    5. Reconciles . . .
    6. Rom. 1:16 . . .

Conclusion. John 5:39

# SALT
## MATT. 5:13-16

Introduction.   Christ regards his people as the "Salt of the earth"—

I.   ITS FUNCTION—to season . . .
   1. To bring out the best flavor . . .
   2. Desired and needed by all . . . (1) Savages trade valuables for small portions . . . (2) Cattle travel long distances for it . . .
   3. The influence of Christianity will develop the best in man . . .

II.   ITS FUNCTION—to preserve . . .
   1. Salt is to preserve from corruption that on which it is sprinkled . . . You must sprinkle enough . . .
   2. The world is in danger of sinking into corruption . . .
      (a) Society threatened with disintegration by opposition of conflicting classes . . . For example, the race problem . . .
      (b) Domestic life is corroded by immorality and intemperance . . .
      (c) Frivolous amusements tend to become unwholesome . . .
      (d) A preserving and purifying agent is needed . . .
   3. The world is worth preserving . . .
      (a) Christ does not desire the destruction of civilization, but its preservation . . . (a) He has power to destroy it . . . (b) He died to save and preserve it . . (c) He commissioned us, His agents and instruments . . .
      (b) Politics, commerce, art, literature, all are worth preserving against corruption . . .

III.   ITS ACTION—salt is an antiseptic—the church is expected to be of the same character . . .
   1. Not merely to be pure—but to purify . . .
   2. Not just during campaigns—but the constant influence of Christians . . . In every day living . . .

IV.   ITS FAILURE . . .
   1. Salt may lose its savor (preserving and seasoning power)—So may the church lose her power to witness . . .
   2. When this happens, it is useless for the intended . . . (1) It is still salt but with no power . . . (2) Used to make roads . . .
   3. When the church loses the spirit of Christ, she becomes a hindrance rather than help—the power is gone . . . The spirit of Christ is LOVE, COMPASSION, RIGHTEOUSNESS . . .
   4. The church is salt—not sugar . . . (1) Sugar will sweeten, but not preserve . . . (2) Sugar will make for pleasant taste, but will not purify . . .

Conclusion.   Do you season that with which you come in contact?

# THE REASON FOR OUR FAILURES
## MATT. 17:14-21

Introduction.  We often see our failures but seldom do we try to find the real reason for them — we always come with an explanation, but is this the reason? What do we do about it?
1. When homes fail, each places the blame on the other—divorce is the result . . .
2. What about juvenile delinquency—What is the cause—What are we doing about it? . . .
3. Business fails, national economy staggers, politics is blamed . . .
4. Crops fail—insects, drouth, etc. . . .
5. When we fail to get rain, there is conversation and complaining about it—some have employed "rain-makers" . . .
6. When our churches fail to meet the expectations in results, we start looking for a new pastor . . .

SOME THINGS WE MUST REMEMBER FROM THE SCRIPTURES:
1. Matt. 19:4-9 . . .
2. Prov. 22:6 . . .
3. II Chron. 7:12-15 . . .
4. James 5:16 . . .
5. Heb. 10:23-25 . . .

Let us rethink the real reason for our failures, and what we should do about it . . . Our text is the example—Matt. 17:14-21 . . .

I.   THE FAILURE—the problem before them . . .
An afflicted boy had been brought to the disciples and they could not heal him—WHY??
1. The father expected the wrong person to heal his son . . .
   (a) The disciples—verse 16 . . .
   (b) It is God, not his ordained, who has miraculous power . . .
2. There was doubt and lack of faith—Mark 9:23, 24 . . .
3. Perverseness—they had turned away from the truth of God . . .
   Perversion of Scripture . . .

II.  THE ANSWER OF THE LORD—verses 20, 21 . . .
1. Unbelief . . .
2. Lack of faith . . .
3. Lack of prayer . . .
4. Lack of fasting . . .
   (a) This means much more than penitence . . .
   (b) It means being more interested in the will of God than in our personal welfare . . .

Conclusion.  We have failed in many categories. Let us go back to Calvary, find the solution, and make a new start.

# HOW TO BECOME CHILDREN
## TEXT, MATT. 18:3 — CONTEXT, JOHN 1:10-13

Introduction. In our text, we find the imperative, "Except ye be converted and become as little children, ye shall not enter into the kingdom of Heaven." This does not mean that one must revert to his infancy and become childish . . . Neither does it mean that we are to become juvenile . . . It *does* mean that one must become humble, teachable, trustful . . . Not doubting, but in faith looking unto the Father . . . To become children of God, one must receive the WORD—the Son of God . . .
Therefore, receive:

I. *HIM* WHO MADE THE WORLD—verse 10
1. He who made the world can easily remake a human soul . . . Make it ready for Heaven . . .
2. His creative power was manifested by His miraculous works . . . (a) Feeding the 5000 . . . (b) Stilling the tempest . . . (c) Raising the dead . . . (d) Healing the sick . . . (e) Forgiving sins . . .

II. *HIM* WHO WAS IN THE WORLD, BUT NOT OF THE WORLD—
1. Took upon himself the form of sinful flesh . . .                              verse 10
2. Lived among sinners but entirely without sin . . .
3. Bore every type of temptation, yet did not yield . . .

III. *HIM* WHO IS THE TRUE LIGHT—verse 9
1. Artificial light is deceptive . . . Notice the difference in colors in artificial and sunlight . . .
2. Verses 4, 5 . . .
3. He is the True Light—True Vine—True Bread . . .
4. To receive Him is to receive the light of life . . .

IV. *HIM* WHO WAS REJECTED BY HIS OWN—verse 11
1. They knew Him as the Son of Joseph—but refused to acknowledge Him as the Son of God . . .
2. They received with eagerness His many blessings—but they did not receive Him . . .
3. No fault found in Him—no accusation of sin—yet was rejected . . .

V. *HIM* WHO HAS AUTHORITY TO MAKE US CHILDREN OF GOD
—verse 12
1. No man—no church—no institution has power and authority to redeem . . . "Ye must be born again"—John 3:3-7 . . .
2. "As many as receive Him" . . . (a) In receiving Him we receive redemption . . . (b) The spirit of adoption . . . (c) Gal. 3:24 . . .

VI. *HIM* WHO HAS POWER TO REGENERATE THE SOUL—verse 13
Regeneration is of God through Christ . . . (a) It is not a natural birth—"Not of blood" . . . Born again—second time—John 3:3-7 . . . (b) Cannot be produced by any amount of fleshly energy—Nor of the will of the flesh . . . (c) Neither can it come by the force of intellectual effort—Nor of the will of man . . . (d) "But of God" . . .

Conclusion. As many as receive Him are born of God. CHRIST IN YOU—the hope of glory.

17.

# BEYOND THIS LIFE
## MATT. 25:32-34, 41, 46

Introduction. In this message we shall endeavor to picture the destinies "beyond this life." 1. The Bible is very clear on the subject—only two . . . (a) Heaven for the redeemed . . . (b) Hell for the unredeemed . . . 2. "It is appointed unto man once to die . . . " . . . 3. Matt. 25:46—text . . ,

I. HEAVEN
  1. Heaven is a place—John 14:2c . . .
     (a) Not a mental state . . .
     (b) A place of residence . . . (1) Jesus came down from Heaven . . . (2) Left the earth and returned to Heaven—Acts 1:8 . . . (3) "Many Mansions" . . .
  2. Heaven is a prepared place—John 14:2 . . .
     (a) Prepared by a person—Jesus . . .
     (b) Prepared beautiful . . .
     (c) Prepared comfortable . . . Rev. 21:4—no tears, sorrows, pain, death . . .
     (d) A prepared place for a prepared people . . . None of Satan's deceptive crowd will be there . . . This is the separation of the wheat and tares . . .
  3. Heaven is a desired place . . .
     (a) Shown by a desire for Christian funerals . . .
     (b) By heathen worship . . .
  4. Heaven is an eternal place . . .
II. HELL
  1. We turn to Luke 16:19-31 where Jesus has drawn back the curtain of time to allow us to see the horrible picture of the destiny of the damned . . .
  2. The Bible is the ONLY authority—this same Jesus who referred to Heaven as a paradise with perfect peace drew this horrible picture of hell . . .
  3. Hell is a literal place of torment . . .
     (a) Not the grave . . .
     (b) Not a state of mind . . .
     (c) Not the punishment while on earth . . .
     (d) A place prepared by the Devil and his angels . . .
  4. No stops between death and Hell . . . Luke 16:22c, 23 . . .
  5. Hell is a place of unutterable suffering . . .
     (a) "Being in torments" . . .
     (b) "I am tormented in this flame" . . .
     (c) "Thou art tormented" . . .
  6. Consciousness in hell . . .
     (a) The soul of man does not cease . . .
     (b) Eternal death—not void of feeling but eternally dying . . .
  7. Hell is eternal punishment . . .
     Wherever the Bible speaks of the hereafter, it is always "eternal," "everlasting," or "never-ending" . . .
III. WHO WILL BE IN HELL?
  1. Rev. 20:15 . . .
  2. John 3:18, 36 . . .
WHERE WILL YOU SPEND ETERNITY??

## AT THE END OF THIS LIFE, WHAT?
### LUKE 17:26-30; I THESS. 4:13-17

Introduction. We are thinking, primarily, of the second coming of Christ— the end of this dispensation. Many fail to understand why we should preach, or study, the second coming; saying, "This has nothing to do with salvation." ALL men will have an interest in the second coming of Christ. The saved will have the rewards of eternal glory; the unsaved, the full impact of the judgment. No man knows the time. We may disagree on the details—none of these will alter the facts—THE LORD IS COMING!!

I. THE FACT OF HIS COMING
    1. 1800 references in the Bible . . . Paul mentions it 50 times—baptism 13 . . .
    2. The testimony of Jesus . . .
    3. Of the angels . . .
    4. Of the Lord's Supper . . .

II. CONDITIONS AT THE TIME OF HIS COMING—Luke 17:26-28
    1. Social and Professional . . . (a) Life will be normal . . . (b) Business as usual . . .
    2. Politically—deception and corruption—I Thess. 5:3 . . .
    3. Morally—corruption and debauchery . . . As in the days of Noah and Lot . . .
    4. Spiritually—Gen. 6:5—"Wickedness of man was great" . . .

III. THE ASPECTS OF HIS COMING—RAPTURE AND REVELATION
    1. The rapture . . .
       (a) Dead in Christ shall rise first—I Thess. 4:16 . . .
       (b) Those alive, caught up in the air—verse 17 . . .
       (c) The unsaved dead will not be disturbed at this time—Rev. 20:5 . . .
       (d) The judgment (manifestation) of works (not salvation)—I Cor. 3:13-15 . . .
    2. The revelation . . .
       (a) The Battle of Armageddon in progress . . .
       (b) Jesus will bring an end to this war—Rev. 19:14, 15 . . .
       (c) With Him shall be all Christians—Rev. 19:14—I Thess. 4:14, 15 . . .
       (d) We shall live and reign with Him a thousand years—Rev. 20:6 . . .

Conclusion. Every person chooses NOW—Christ or the Anti-Christ. (1) Those belonging to Christ will be in Heaven with Him eternally. (2) Those of the Anti-Christ will be in Hell with him eternally.

WHAT IS YOUR CHOICE??

# CALVARY
## LUKE 23:33

Introduction. Let us look at Calvary—the most sacred place in the world.

CALVARY—where the Son of God died that the sons of men might live.

CALVARY—where the innocent blood of Jesus was shed to cleanse us all.

CALVARY—where all the sin of the world was laid on one who knew no sin.

CALVARY—where men can come with their troubles and find the peace which passeth all understanding.

CALVARY—where you and I receive life, joy, and assurance.

CALVARY—where Jesus paid it all.

I.  AT CALVARY WE SEE THE LOVE AND COMPASSION OF JESUS "FATHER FORGIVE THEM."
1. Those who crucified Him . . .
2. Those who mocked Him . . .
3. Those who tempted Him . . .
4. Those who were indifferent . . .
5. Those who deny Him . . .
6. Those who reject Him—prayer for their salvation . . .

II.  AT CALVARY WE SEE THE PERFECT PICTURE OF SALVATION BY GRACE, *ALONE*
1. The thief had nothing to offer the Lord, either before or after this hour . . . Just as he was . . .
2. This refutes the idea of works—ceremony—creeds—etc. . . .
3. The thief did only two things . . .
   (a) Repented . . .
   (b) Trusted . . .

III.  AT CALVARY WE HEAR THE PROMISE TO ALL WHO COME "TODAY SHALT THOU BE WITH ME IN PARADISE."
1. We have done nothing to merit even his attention . . .
2. Instantaneous salvation . . .
3. Companionship with the Son of God . . . This denotes perfection (spiritual) . . . Not our righteousness—*BUT HIS* . . .
4. "Paradise"—"The Paradise of God" . . .

IV.  AT CALVARY WE HEAR THE WORDS "IT IS FINISHED" . . .
1. Salvation is within reach of all people . . .
2. Salvation is completed—nothing to be added . . . Just accept as a gift . . .

Conclusion.  "Jesus paid it all, all to Him I owe,
  Sin has left a crimson stain, He washed it white as snow."

COME TO CALVARY, IN FAITH!

# WERE YOU THERE WHEN THEY CRUCIFIED MY LORD?
## LUKE 23:33-38

Introduction. The Negro spiritual, "Were You There When They Crucified My Lord?" . . . (1) The thoughtless answer is "*NO!* No living person could have been." (2) The spiritual is insistent—"*Were You There?*"—Many were.

I. NICODEMUS WAS THERE—in all his judicial pride
1. The man who went to Jesus to inquire of salvation . . . who recognized Jesus as Rabbi (Master) . . . who later helped to bury the Lord . . . who was not ready to face persecution and ridicule . . . stood by in his pride and said nothing . . .
2. If you let pride rule any part of your life and prevent your serving the Master, YOU WERE THERE.

II. JUDAS ISCARIOT WAS THERE—led there by greed
1. Greed caused Judas to sell the Master for 30 pieces of silver . . . to cry out against the woman who anointed Jesus . . . to betray the Son of God while moving under the guise of friendship . . .
2. Greed causes wars—depressions—corruption of nations, etc. . . . causes people to rob God of that which belongs to Him . . .
3. Yes! Greed was there when they crucified my Lord . . .

III. PETER WAS THERE
1. In Gethsemane he drew a sword to defend Jesus—while Jesus was near . . . followed afar off . . . denied Jesus three times out of fear . . .
2. Jesus is hurt when professing Christians deny the Lord in word and deed . . . (a) He was crushed when the apostles fled . . . (b) When Peter denied him . . .
3. Yes, fear, cowardice, and neglect were there . . .

IV. THE CHIEF PRIESTS WERE THERE—in all their ecclesiastical dignity . . . Preferring the church to the Saviour . . .

V. THE PHARISEES WERE THERE—with their formal worship . . . II Tim. 3:5 . . . 1. Preferring tradition to the Word of God . . . 2. Destroying Christ rather than yield to His power . . .

VI. THEN THERE WAS A HOST OF INDIFFERENT PEOPLE, NOT IDENTIFIED—Indifference is probably the heaviest anchor attached to Christianity today . . .

VII. THERE WAS STILL ANOTHER INDIVIDUAL STANDING BY THE CROSS—the Centurion.
1. He had witnessed the miracle of restoration of the severed ear in Gethsemane . . . heard the prayer and other words of Jesus on the cross . . . saw something much more than a man dying on the cross . . . saw and recognized the redeeming blood pouring forth . . . He saw a personal Saviour . . . "Surely this was the Son of God" . . .
2. Many witnesses to Christ's power were there . . .

VIII. WERE YOU THERE WHEN THEY CRUCIFIED THE LORD?
Not physically—but because of our sins the Lord was crucified . . . Our sins of pride, greed, cowardice, neglect, fear, ecclesiastical dignity and formalism, indifference, blindness to God's power, nailed him there.

Conclusion. YES! We were all there—"All we like sheep have gone astray—" As our sins were gathered at the cross of our Lord to crucify Him—so must we return to the cross to be delivered from our sin.
THERE IS A FOUNTAIN FILLED WITH BLOOD!

# REMEMBER HIS WORDS
## LUKE 24:1-12

Introduction. Text, v. 8 "They remembered His words about His passion."
. . . Let us remember His words:

I. ABOUT GOD'S LOVE AND CARE
   1. John 3:16 . . .
   2. I Peter 5:7 . . .
   3. Luke 12:6, 7 . . .

II. ABOUT PRAYER
   1. The model prayer—adoration, confession, petition—Matt. 6:9-12 . . .
   He added verses 14, 15 . . .
   2. John 14:13, 14 . . .
   3. James 5:16b . . .

III. ABOUT HEAVEN
   1. The dwelling place of God the Father . . .
   2. Future home of the saints . . .
   John 14:2—Matt. 25:34 . . .
   3. To the thief on the cross—Paradise . . .

IV. ABOUT HELL
   1. Jesus had more to say about Hell than about Heaven . . .
   2. He described the place . . .
   3. Warned against going there . . .
   4. The picture—Luke 16:19-31 (Dives and Lazarus) . . .

V. ABOUT PREPARATION AND ETERNITY
   1. Amos 4:12 . . .
   2. Building on sand or rock . . .
   3. Matt. 24:44 . . .
   4. Parable of 10 virgins . . .
   5. A horrible picture—Matt. 24:35-42 . . .

Conclusion. "Remember His Words" . . .
   1. Has made provisions for this life and the life to come . . .
   2. Has described the destinies . . .
   3. He invites you . . .
   4. Has then left the decision with you . . .

WHAT IS YOUR RESPONSE?

22

# JOHN'S TESTIMONY OF CHRIST
## JOHN 1:29-34

Introduction. John the Baptist, the forerunner of Christ, had a testimony of Christ that he was first, last, and always.

I.  HE IS THE LAMB OF GOD—verse 29
   1. God's chosen Lamb to bear away the sin of the world . . .
   2. The Lamb slain from the foundation of the world . . .
   3. The fufillment of the passover lamb . . .
      (a) Prophecy of the blood covering . . .
      (b) The lamb without spot or blemish . . .

II.  HE IS THE ETERNAL CHRIST—verse 30
   1. He was before all things . . .
      "Before Abraham was, I am." . . .
   2. He is before all things . . .
      "For in Him we live, and move, and have our being."
      Acts 17:28 . . .
   3. The Alpha and Omega . . .
   4. The creator and the great judge . . .

III.  HE IS PREFERRED BEFORE ME—verse 30
   1. In all things He must have pre-eminence . . .
   2. When He has first place in our lives, we have the best of His blessings . .

IV.  HE IS THE ANOINTED ONE—verse 32
   1. The Father said, "Thou art my beloved son" . . .
      John was witness to this . . .
   2. Anointed for the specific purpose to provide redemption . . .

V.  HE IS THE SON OF GOD—verse 34
   1. As the lamb, He put away sin by the sacrifice of himself . . .
   2. As the Son, He is almighty to save . . .
      "All power is given unto me" . . .
   3. The Son of God who bore the temptation . . .
   4. The Son of God who loved enough to give all . . .

Conclusion. He is the Christ, the Son of the living God—He is the Saviour to all who come unto God by Him.

WHAT IS YOUR TESTIMONY OF THE CHRIST?

# DISCIPLES OF CHRIST
## JOHN 1:35-42

Introduction. What does it mean to be a disciple of Christ? The word "disciple" is defined as . . . (a) One who *receives* instruction—a learner . . . (b) One who *follows* the teachings, examples, and precepts of another . . . (c) Scripture, John 8:31 . . . John 15:8 . . . (d) Jesus made "love one for another" a mark of discipleship . . . There are five steps to discipleship. They are:

I. RECOGNITION OF CHRIST
   1. As the Lamb of God which taketh away the sin of the world . . .
   2. As the one who is able to save to the uttermost . . .
   3. As the one worth forsaking all else for . . .
   4. As the one to be trusted and followed . . .
   5. John recognized Him and bore testimony that He was the Son of God . . . *He is God* . . .

II. AN ACT OF FAITH—verse 37
   1. They heard and they believed . . .
   2. To believe is one thing—to follow is another . . .
   3. Action is the evidence of faith . . .
   4. "Faith cometh by hearing and hearing by the Word of God" . . .

III. A HEART-SEARCHING QUESTION—verse 38—"WHAT SEEK YE?"
   1. Jesus will test the motives of those who call upon Him . . .
   2. What seek ye? What do you expect out of following Jesus? . . .
      (a) Worldly honor and preference . . .
      (b) Material gifts? . . .
      (c) Influence for self-exaltation . . .
   3. Or, do you seek Christ as Saviour and Guide? . . .
      (a) "I am the way"—The way to God and righteous living . . .
      (b) "I am the truth"—The truth of sin, righteousness, judgment . . .
   4. This question will search our hearts—"What seek ye?" . . . Are we more anxious to be honored by Christ than to honor Him? . . . "If any man follow me, let him deny himself"—Matt. 16:24 . . .

IV. A GRACIOUS INVITATION
   1. "They said unto Him, Master, where dwellest thou? He said unto them, come and see."—verses 38, 39 . . .
   2. They accepted His invitation and "came and saw where He dwelt, and abode with Him" . . .
   3. His invitation says . . . (a) Come . . . (b) Receive . . (c) Follow . . .

V. A WILLING SERVICE
   1. Andrew findeth his own brother, Simon, and he brought him to Jesus . . .
   2. True disciples of Christ will be fruit-bearing witnesses . . .
   3. John 15:8 . . .

Conclusion.
   1. We must follow Him as Saviour and trust Him . . .
   2. We must follow Him as our Guide . . .

ARE YOU A FOLLOWER OF CHRIST—A TRUE DISCIPLE??

# CLEANSING THE TEMPLE
## JOHN 2:13-21

Introduction. There is a striking contrast between the scene at the marriage (verse 1) and that at the passover in Jerusalem . . . (1) At one, He was an invited guest; at the other an unwelcomed stranger although the Temple was His Father's house . . . (2) In one, He wrought a miracle of grace; in the other, a miracle of judgment . . . (3) In one picture, He is supplying a need; in the other, He is meting out justice . . . Let us note:

I. THE TRUE CHARACTER OF THE TEMPLE
  1. Jesus calls it "My Father's House" . . . (a) Dedicated to the service of God . . . (b) Identified with the name of God . . . (c) As such, God is the supreme head . . .
  2. A house of prayer . . . (a) Not a commercial market . . . (b) Reverence —not confusion . . . (c) Harmony—not dissension . . .

II. HOW THE TEMPLE WAS DEFILED
  1. Defiled by those who professed to be but were not friends of the Temple . . .
  2. Defiled by allowing worldliness to come into the Temple . . . through (1) unregenerate members . . . (2) compromise with Satan . . .
  3. Defiled from within, not from without . . .

III. HOW CHRIST IS TREATED IN A DEFILED TEMPLE
  1. His name is used as a shield to cover sin . . .
  2. He is given lip service to impress men . . .
  3. They have "a form of Godliness, but deny the power thereof" II Tim. 3:5 . . .
  4. Honor and reverence for Christ is swallowed up in arrogance, greed, selfishness . . .

IV. HOW THE TEMPLE WAS CLEANSED
  1. Cleansed by the incoming of the Master himself . . . His presence means purity, righteousness . . .
  2. The defilers were driven out . . . (a) Not by physical force . . . (b) by His presence and power . . . Sometimes it becomes necessary for God to take drastic measures to cleanse the Temple . . .

V. THE SIGN OF HIS AUTHORITY AS A CLEANSER—The Resurrection, verse 8.
  1. His resurrection is evidence of power and authority . . . (a) To cleanse our hearts . . . (b) To cleanse the Temple . . .
  2. His resurrection is our assurance of resurrection . . .

Conclusion. Be not deceived—God will either cleanse the Temple or He will destroy it . . . (1) Temple in Jerusalem destroyed in 70 A. D. . . . (2) Those who reject Christ will be destroyed . . .

# GOD'S LETTER TO MANKIND
## JOHN 3:14-18

Introduction. If there is any text that Satan would like to blot out of the Bible, it is John 3:16 . . . If there is any text that has made the foundation pillars of hell tremble, it is John 3:16 . . . If there is any text that has lightened up the pathway of Heaven for the multitudes of men, it is John 3:16 . . . If there is any text that deserves to be called "the little Bible," it is John 3:16 . . . This verse, spoken to Nicodemus, embodies the whole truth of God's love and His infinite plan of redemption . . . It is world-wide in scope, yet it is a personal letter to every individual . . .

I. THIS LETTER FROM GOD IS A LOVE LETTER
   1. The writer of this letter is GOD . . . The creator and divine lover of our souls . . .
   2. The subject of this letter is LOVE . . . Love is deep concern for our welfare and needs . . .

II. GOD'S LETTER IS WRITTEN IN CRIMSON INK—"HE GAVE HIS ONLY BEGOTTEN SON"
   1. Peter says—I Peter 1:19 . . . John says—I John 1:7 . . . Paul says—Rom. 5:9 . . . The redeemed in Heaven sing—Rev. 5:9 . . . Jesus himself said—Matt. 26:28 . . .
   2. One third of the Gospels is devoted to the sacrifice of Christ (the passion week) . . .
   3. Think of the sacrifice of Christ—no part of His body escaped suffering . . .
      (a) His hands and His feet were pierced with nails . . .
      (b) His temples were lacerated with thorns . . .
      (c) His tongue clave to His jaws . . .
      (d) His throat was parched with thirst . . .
      (e) His back was torn with the scourge . . .
      (f) His side was pierced with the spear . . .
      (g) His bones were all disjointed . . .
      (h) His muscles were stretched in agony . . .
      (i) His nerves became rivers of anguish . . .
      (j) His great heart broke under the load of your sin and mine . . .
   4. Was it any wonder that the "earth did quake and the rocks rent"? . . .

III. THE CONTENTS OF SUBJECT OF THIS LETTER
   1. Offers eternal life . . .
   2. The one condition of this offer is "Believe in Him" . . .
   3. This offer mentions two alternatives . . . (a) Everlasting life . . . (b) Everlasting death (perish) . . .

IV. TO WHOM IS THIS LETTER ADDRESSED?
   1. "Whosoever" . . .
   2. A personal letter to you . . .

Conclusion. Here is God's letter to you telling of the crimson blood that was shed for the remission of sin—the offer of eternal life. Your acceptance, or rejection, of this offer determines your destiny.
WHAT IS YOUR ANSWER?

# THE LIVING WATER
## JOHN 4:7-14

Introduction. These words of Jesus about the "living water" spoken as they were to a sinful Samaritan are deeper and more lasting than the well of Jacob. Jacob's well had been giving fresh, life-sustaining water for some 1800 years—the water Jesus spake of was everlasting.

I. THE NATURE OF THE LIVING WATER
    1. It is life-giving—not just life-sustaining . . .
    2. It is water which saves and satisfies . . .

II. THE SOURCE OF IT
    1. verse 10 . . .
        (a) Jesus is the disposer of this "living water" . . .
        (b) John 17:2 . . .
    2. This water of "grace and truth" came by the Son of God . . .
        (a) The need of the Samaritan woman . . .
        (b) The *Truth* as the Lord exposed her sin . . .
        (c) Grace offered life . . .

III. THE EFFICACY OF IT
    1. It quenches thirst . . .
    Never thirst for the muddy waters of sin . . .
    2. It becomes a spring within—verse 14 . . .
        (a) The heart of the earth yields crystal clear, pure water through the spring . . .
        (b) The temptations of the regenerated man are like the poisonous berries that drop into the spring—are soon purified by the pure waters that come from within . . .

IV. THE CONDITIONS OF THE LIVING WATER
    1. "If thou knewest the gift of God, thou wouldest have asked Him" . . .
    2. Acknowledging the power of Christ . . .
    3. Asking of Him . . .
    "Ask and ye shall receive" . . .

V. THE FREENESS OF IT—verse 14
    1. Rev. 22:17 . . .
    2. Isa. 55:1 . . .

Conclusion. Jesus said, "If any man thirst, let him come unto me and drink." —John 7:37.

# WHEN JESUS COMES
## JOHN 4:25

Introduction. When Jesus came into the world as a babe in Bethlehem's manger, the world was very much the same as it is today . . . (1) Some loved God and lived righteously . . . (2)Some gave themselves wholly to sin . . . (3) Corruption on every hand . . . (4) He came into a world greatly in need of spiritual life and guidance . . . (5)When Jesus comes it means the difference between . . . (a) Heaven and hell . . . (b) Happiness and misery . . . (c) Salvation and damnation . . .

I. WHEN HE COMES TO BEHOLD THE SIN AND CORRUPTION IN OUR LIVES, AND IN OUR CITIES—*HE WEEPS*—Luke 19:41

   1. He sees the sin that we sometimes overlook . . .
   2. He weeps—not because it hurts Him personally, but because sin destroys the souls of men . . . As the person who loses something that is cherished . . .

II. WHEN HE COMES TO US, IN CONVICTION, HE WILL TELL US ALL THINGS—John 4:25

   1. He amazed the woman by exposing to her her past . . .
   2. Conviction makes the "best" moral man to know how much he needs Christ . . . Compared to His righteousness, we have very little . . .

III. WHEN HE COMES INTO OUR HEARTS BY FAITH, WE HAVE A CLEAR CONCEPT OF CHRIST, AND PEACE THAT PASSETH UNDERSTANDING—I John 5:20 . . .

   1. In conviction we see and know our need—in Christ we have our need supplied . . .
   2. We may not understand how we are saved—but we know we are saved . . . This assurance comes only when we are completely surrendered . . .
   3. We know Him as Saviour . . . (a) As the guide in life . . . (b) The provider of all necessities . . .
   4. Every sin is forgiven . . . Heb. 8:12 . . .
   5. Our desires and ambitions are new . . . Likewise our attitudes . . .

IV. WHEN HE COMES AGAIN—ALL WILL BE PERFECT—I Cor. 13:10 . . .

   1. We will be with Jesus . . .
   2. Satan will be bound and cast into the bottomless pit . . .
   3. Sin will be put down . . .
   4. The ungodly perished from the earth . . .
   5. Afterwards will come the perfect judgment . . .

Conclusion

   1. Jesus came and gave His life to save us . . .
   2. He is here, in the person of the Holy Spirit, convicting . . .
   3. He wants you to let Him come into your heart—by faith . . .
   4. That He might come to receive you unto the Father after this life . . .

HE WANTS YOU TO RECEIVE HIM—TRUST HIM—FOLLOW HIS COMMANDMENTS!

# SALVATION ACCORDING TO CHRIST
## JOHN 5:21-29

Introduction.

1. Salvation must come from the Son—John 5:21 . . .
   (a) Not from a ceremony, however sacred . . .
   (b) Not from a system of laws, however perfect . . .
   (c) But from a person, the Son, the Saviour . . .
2. If one has not the Son he has not life, but the wrath of God abides upon him—John 3:34-36 . . .
3. How then, may one receive the Son and come into eternal life? . . .

FOUR THINGS ARE MENTIONED HERE BY THE MASTER

I. HEARING—verse 24

1. No case in the New Testament of anyone being saved without hearing the Word . . .
   (a) This hearing implies recognition of the Word as a message from God for the soul . . .
   (b) Hearing produces conviction of sin . . .
2. Paul is just as explicit as is Jesus in this message . . .
   Rom. 10:14-17 . . .
   "Faith cometh from hearing, and hearing by the Word of God."

II. BELIEVING—verse 24

1. Here again the New Testament is never changed or broken . . .
   Always it is, "He that believeth" . . .
2. Again the Apostle Paul reinforces the message of the Master—
   Rom. 10:8-15 . . .
3. John 3:14-18 . . .

III. RECEIVING—verse 24

1. John 1:11-12 . . .
2. To receive Him is to surrender unto His own . . .
3. Faith that He is able to save and to guide . . .
4. John 3:36 . . .

IV. EXPERIENCING—PASSING OVER—verse 24d

1. New life has come into the believer's soul—a new creature in Christ Jesus . . .
2. This cannot be explained; it must be experienced . . .

Conclusion. Here is the completed transaction—hearing, believing, receiving, and experiencing.

1. Have you received the Son of God?
2. Have you experienced the infilling of the Holy Spirit, implanting a new life? . . .
3. Christ alone can save.

WILL YOU RECEIVE HIM??

# JESUS CAME
## JOHN 6:32-40

Introduction. The Incarnation of the Eternal Son, involving the virgin birth of the Lord Jesus Christ, was a plan conceived in the mind of the infinite before the dawn of creation.

HE CAME!

I. NOT TO REFORM, BUT TO TRANSFORM
1. Reformation is very fine in its place, but is not sufficient . . . That is not our need . . .
2. Definition of reform . . .
    (a) To make better or return to a former good state . . .
    (b) To amend—correct . . .
3. Our need is not physical or moral, but is spiritual . . .
4. Transforms the soul now—the body in eternity . . .

II. NOT TO REPAIR, BUT TO REPLACE
1. Like repairing an old automobile or house . . . It is still the same—just patched up with a new coat of paint . . .
2. Jesus came to replace our sinful nature with spiritual nature . . .
    (a) A new heart . . .
    (b) New attitudes . . .
    (c) New outlook . . .

III. NOT TO SAVE US FROM WRONG-DOING, BUT TO SAVE US
                                   FROM WRONG-BEING
1. We are by nature children of Satan . . .
2. By birth, sinners . . .
3. We do wrong because we are wrong . . .
4. We are by nature the "children of wrath"—Eph. 2:3 . . .
5. Without Christ you are the "living dead" . . . Alive in the flesh—dead spiritually . . .

IV. HE CAME TO BRING LIFE
1. Natural men are dead in trespasses and sins . . .
2. John 10:10 . . .
3. He brought life by overcoming death . . .
4. Physical life is in the blood of your veins . . .
5. Spiritual life is in the blood of Christ . . .

V. HE CAME TO DO THE WILL OF THE FATHER
1. The Father's will is that men should be saved . . .
2. That the Son should keep them without losing even one . . .
3. That He should raise them up again at the last day . . .

Conclusion. Jesus came to give you life—He is coming to receive you.

# TO WHOM SHALL WE GO?
## JOHN 6:37-40, 63-69

Introduction. The sixth chapter of John records the feeding of the 5000; the miracle of Jesus walking on the water . . .

The next day people came seeking Jesus. Their motives were wrong. Jesus warned them against worldliness and offered them spiritual food—"My Father giveth you the true bread from Heaven—I am the bread of life"—verses 32, 35 . . .

After this discourse many went back and walked with him no more.

Let us note the crowds following Jesus and their respective attitudes:
1. Some of curiosity—these did not "stick" . . .
2. Some for loaves and fishes—these did not "stick" . . .
3. Some because of their need—some "stuck" . . .
4. Some because of their love—these "stuck" . . .

TO WHOM SHALL WE GO?

I. WE MUST HAVE SOMEONE TO WHOM WE CAN GO
  1. In life . . .
      (a) With problems—someone who can give advice . . .
      (b) With fears—someone who can protect . . .
      (c) With sins—Someone who can forgive . . .
  2. In death . . .
      (a) To whom shall we go in the loss of a loved one? . . .
      (b) As we face death ourselves . . .
  3. On the Judgment Day . . .
      (a) We must have an advocate . . .
      (b) We have nothing of ourselves to offer . . .

II. WE CAN GO TO NO ONE BUT JESUS
  1. Shall we go to our governor? . . .
  2. Shall we go to our educators? . . .
  3. Shall we go to our friends and loved ones? These would help if they could . . .

III. WE CAN GO TO JESUS
  1. He can help in every case . . .
  2. God has given Him all authority and power . . .
  3. He paid for our sins on the cross . . .
  4. He died and rose again that we may fear death no longer . . .
  5. He is our advocate before God . . .
  6. He invites us to come . . .

Conclusion.
  1. You need medical attention—you go to a doctor . . .
  2. Legal advice—a lawyer . . .
  3. Salvation—the Saviour . . .

# THE ETERNAL HOME OF THE REDEEMED
## JOHN 14:1-6 — ACTS 1:10, 11 — REV. 21:1-4

Introduction.
1. When anticipating a change of residence, we want to know something of the new location . . .
2. We shall all change our abode at the end of this life . . .
3. There are two choices—Heaven and hell . . . The choice must be made in this life . . .
4. We consider Heaven . . . What is Heaven and where is it? . . .
5. How can we know there is a Heaven? . . . The illustration of the little boy and his kite: We can feel the tug of Heaven; the urge of the Holy Spirit to turn to Christ should convince us that Heaven is a reality . . .

I. HEAVEN IS A PLACE—"I go to prepare *a place*" . . .
1. Some say, "Heaven is a mental state" . . .
2. A place of residence . . .
   (a) Jesus came down from Heaven . . .
   (b) Went back to the Father . . .
   (c) "In my Father's house are many mansions" . . .

II. HEAVEN IS A PREPARED PLACE—"I go to *prepare*"
1. Prepared by a person . . . By Christ himself . . .
2. Prepared big enough . . .
3. Prepared beautiful . . .
   (a) As represented by the stones—Rev. 21 . . .
   (b) We see the outside (Second Heaven)—the moon, etc. . . .
   (c) Contrasted with outer darkness of hell . . .
4. Prepared comfortable . . .
   (a) Rev. 21:4—no tears, sorrow, etc. . . .
   (b) Contrasted with "wailing and gnashing of teeth" . . .
5. A prepared place for a prepared people . . .

III. HEAVEN IS A BUSY PLACE
1. All will be busy singing, praising, and serving God . . .
2. No time for lazy Christians . . .

IV. HEAVEN IS A PLACE OF CHRISTIAN FELLOWSHIP
1. The people there are the ones who are true Christians . . .
2. None of the Devil's deceptive crowd . . .
3. The separation of the wheat and the tares . . .

V. HEAVEN IS A DESIRED PLACE
1. Shown by desire for Christian funerals . . .
2. By heathen worship . . .
3. Testified to in last minute statements . . .

VI. HEAVEN IS AN ETERNAL PLACE—John 14:1-6—ONLY ONE WAY TO HEAVEN!

# THE UNAVOIDABLE CHRIST
## JOHN 20:19-31

Introduction. Let us go upstairs and visit in the upper room . . .
1. Locked doors but Jesus stood in the midst . . .
2. Our message concerns the crucified and risen Son of God . . .
The Living Christ that will not be avoided . . .

I. JESUS CHRIST IS A PERSON
1. Biblical history refers to Him from the beginning . . .
2. Profane history, apart from the Bible, verifies His existence along with Julius Caesar, Nero, Constantine, and others . . .
3. The date on the coin tells that Christ lived . . . Would the world's calendar be based on the birthday of a man who never lived? . . .
4. Not even the Jews, as a nation, will deny the existence of Jesus . . .

II. HE IS A UNIQUE PERSON
1. Unique in His birth . . . Born of a virgin, therefore without sin . . .
2. Unique in His life . . .
3. Unique in His claims and power . . . (a) One with the Father . . . (b) He spoke with authority . . . (c) He forgave sins and restored lives . . . (d) Had power over natural laws—even locked doors . . .
4. Unique in His death . . . (a) He died praying for others . . . (b) He died at the hands of others . . . (c) He died because of others . . .

III. HE IS AN UNAVOIDABLE PERSON
1. You may shut Him out of your life, but He will still speak to your heart . . .
2. You may leave Him out of your plans, only to find that He is there . . .
3. Sometimes Christ stands in the midst of adversity . . . Sometimes He enters through sickness . . . Sometimes He enters through the death of a loved one . . .
4. NO! You can't shut Him out! . . .
(a) Some compliment Him as a fine man, a prophet . . .
(b) Some crucify Him—neglect is to crucify Him . . .
5. The inevitable is to meet Christ . . .
If a man could avoid Him in life, He must meet Him in death . . .

Every man must do one of three things with Christ . . .
1. Compliment Him—infidels can do this . . .
2. Crucify Him—every man who rejects Him does this . . .
3. Accept Him—this is what God wants everyone to do . . .

WHAT WILL YOU DO WITH JESUS??

# THE PASSION
## ACTS 1:3 — MATT. 27:33-54 — ISA. 53

Introduction.  The Black Hills "Passion Play" . . .

1. The word "passion" comes from the Latin meaning "to suffer" . . .
2. The sacrificial suffering of Christ, for the sin of the world, is the theme of the Bible . . . Luke 24:46-48 . . .
3. The suffering of Christ began in Gethsemane . . .
   (a) Was continued in Pilate's Hall . . .
   (b) Climaxed on Calvary's Cross . . .

Let us turn to Matthew 27 and analyze a portion of the record of and the results of His suffering.

I. THE CHRIST ON THE CROSS—Matt. 27:33-38
   1. The Christ on the cross died—God's gift to the world, the sacrifice for sin . . .
   2. The Christ of the cross is alive . . . Our Saviour . . .
   3. Seven sentences spoken from the cross—these are seven windows to the heart of Christ . . .
      (a) Luke 23:34 . . . Pleading for lost souls . . .
      (b) John 19:26, 27 . . . Provision for those He loved . . .
      (c) Luke 23:43 . . . Assurance of salvation . . .
      (d) Matt. 27:46 . . . Dependent upon Divine power . . .
      (e) John 19:28 . . . Agony in bearing our sins . . .
      (f) John 19:30 . . . (1) Law fulfilled . . . (2) Salvation complete . . .
      (g) Luke 23:46 . . . Signifying another life after this . . .

II. THE MOCKING CROWDS—Matt. 27:39-44 . . . All of this added to His suffering . . .

III. THE CONFESSION OF THE CENTURION—verse 54
   The result of His suffering . . .
   1. Conviction of sin . . .
      (a) As they watched Jesus die they were burdened at the knowledge of this sacrifice . . .
      (b) The misery of condemnation was felt . . .
      (c) There was terror in their hearts . . .
   2. Confession of Christ . . .
      (a) "Truly was this the Son of God" . . .
      (b) The *Son of God*—with all power . . .
      (c) Power to still the tempest . . .
      (d) To silence Satan . . .
      (e) To call the elements to witness . . .
      (f) To heal broken bodies—to restore life . . .
      (g) To forgive sins—Eternal Life . . .

Conclusion.  See Him now, on the cross—*suffering, dying for you.* See Him now, at the throne of grace—*calling you.*
DO YOU BELIEVE HIM TO BE THE SON OF GOD? WILL YOU RECEIVE HIM NOW AS YOUR SAVIOUR?

# SAVED THROUGH FAITH
## ACTS 16:31 — JOHN 20:29

Introduction.

1. This passage was Paul's answer to the Philippian jailer . . .
   (a) He realized a need . . .
   (b) Was convicted of sin . . .
   (c) Trusted the Christ who had delivered them . . .
   (d) Was saved through his faith . . .
2. The second passage was the Lord's words to Thomas in the upper room . . .
   (a) Thomas was not present at the first meeting . . .
   (b) Refused to believe their testimony that Jesus was alive because he had not seen Him . . .
   (c) When Thomas saw the Lord, he believed . . .

THE WORDS OF JESUS ARE THE ONES WE ARE CONSIDERING—John 20:29 . . . THOSE WHO SEE NOT, YET BELIEVE, ARE MOST BLESSED BECAUSE:

I.  THEIR FAITH IS REAL AND GENUINE
Faith which depends upon sight is not faith . . . Hebrews 11:1 . . .

II.  THEIRS IS A FAITH WHICH HONORS CHRIST
1. Because it is satisfied with the evidence of His resurrection . . .
2. Their faith sees Him as sufficient . . .

III.  IT IS FAITH WHICH HONORS THE WORD
1. The whole world hangs upon the Word of God . . .
2. The Word clearly describes man . . .
   (a) Without Christ, LOST . . .
   (b) In desperate need of salvation . . .
3. The Word points to Christ and salvation . . . John 20:31 (read) . . .

IV.  IT IS A FAITH WHICH LEADS TO SIGHT, TO SPIRITUAL VISION
1. When Thomas believed he saw Christ for what He really was . . . "My Lord and my God" . . .
2. The believer sees more on his knees than the non-believer of keenest intellect can discern by standing on tiptoe . . .

V.  THEIRS IS A FAITH WHICH LEADS TO JUSTIFICATION AND SALVATION

Conclusion. "Believe on the Lord Jesus Christ, and thou shalt be saved." Acts 16:31

# ALL THE TRUTH
## ACTS 20:25-32 — TEXT, ACTS 20:27

Introduction. Paul's last visit to the church at Ephesus was punctuated with the warning, "Your soul is now in your own hands" . . . "You have not heeded the Gospel" . . . "My hands are clean, my conscience is clear" . . . "I have told you the whole truth without compromise" . . .

I. THE WHOLE TRUTH ABOUT GOD
   1. The righteousness of God . . .
   2. The love of God . . .
   3. The patience of God . . .
   4. Also the wrath of God . . .

II. THE WHOLE TRUTH ABOUT SIN
   1. Not simply an error that will be overlooked in ignorance . . .
   2. No lasting pleasure—it has its regrets . . .
   3. Sin is transgression of God's law . . . Breaks the heart of God . . .
   4. All are sinners, and condemned before God . . .
   5. Sin destroys both body and soul . . .
   6. Sin is both a condition and an act . . .
      (a) The unredeemed condition of the soul . . .
      (b) The willful act of the individual . . .

III. THE WHOLE TRUTH ABOUT DEATH
   1. Death is not the end . . . Cessation of earthly activities . . .
   2. Death is certain and without warning . . .
   3. Death closes the curtain to God's mercy . . . No second chance at salvation . . .
   4. Death may be both spiritual and physical . . .

IV. THE WHOLE TRUTH ABOUT HELL, ABOUT JUDGMENT
   1. Hell, like death, is an unpleasant subject, but a certain reality . . .
   2. The Bible speaks more of Hell than of Heaven . . .
   3. Many questions about Hell . . .
      (a) Where is it?
      (b) What is it?
      (c) Is it real or figurative?
      (d) Who will go there?
   4. The judgment is the commitment of the unredeemed into Hell . . .

V. THE WHOLE TRUTH ABOUT SALVATION
   1. The supreme need of every individual . . .
   2. Provided through the love of God . . .
   3. Completed by the Son of God on Calvary . . .
   4. Available ONLY through Christ . . .
   5. Secured ONLY through faith . . .
   6. Kept by the power of God . . .

Conclusion. Here is all the truth . . . *What will you do with it?*

# THE GOSPEL
## ROM. 1:16

Introduction. "I am not ashamed of the gospel"—Rom. 1:16
1. Not a new subject, neither is it hurt with age . . . Men in every generation have heard of it and yet it is as new as tomorrow . . .
2. The meaning of the gospel . . .
   (a) Webster—"The announcement of the salvation of mankind through Jesus Christ" . . .
   (b) The gospel of peace—Eph. 6:15 . . .
   (c) A glorious gospel—II Cor. 4:4 . . .
   (d) A universal gospel—Matt. 24:14 . . .
   (e) An everlasting gospel—Rev. 14:6 . . .
3. The facts of the gospel are—death, burial, and resurrection of Jesus—I Cor. 15:1-4 . . .
   (a) All gospel subjects are related to these facts . . .
   (b) The gospel denounces sin only because the death of Christ atones for sin . . .
   (c) The gospel declares hope because of the resurrection of Jesus . . .

I. THE GOSPEL—ITS PURPOSE
1. To save the lost—"He shall save his people" . . .
2. To abolish death and bring life and immortality to light . . . I Cor. 15:22 . . . John 11:25, 26 . . .
3. To prepare us for the judgment—I Peter 4:17 . . .

II. ITS POWER
1. God's power to salvation—Rom. 1:16 . . . Through the preaching—I Cor. 1:12 . . .
2. The power of the gospel is manifest in a holy life . . .
3. It moves men—I Thess. 1:5 . . . No one remains neutral when they hear . . .

III. ITS DEMANDS
1. That we come—Matt. 11:28 . . .
2. That we go—Matt. 28:19 . . .
3. That we preach—Matt. 10:7 . . .
   (a) In the lives we live . . .
   (b) In our conversation . . .
   (c) In the company we keep . . .
   (d) In our activities . . .
4. "Whatsoever thou doest, do all to the glory of God" . . .

IV. ITS PROMISES
1. They are great and precious—II Peter 1:4 . . .
2. Grace sufficient for every situation—II Cor. 12:9 . . .
3. Divine care and comfort . . .
4. All our needs . . .
5. Divine companionship . . .
6. Remission of sins . . .
7. Adoption into God's family—Gal. 4:5 . . .
8. Eternal life—John 3:16; 10:28 . . .
9. The second coming of Christ . . .
10. The Resurrection—to be with Christ forever . . .

Conclusion. Your decision now means life or death—blessings or cursings—companionship or condemnation—hope or hopelessness—Rom. 1:16.

# FACING THE FACTS BEFORE A JUST GOD
## ROM. 3:9-20 — REV. 20:12-15 — TEXT, ROM. 14:12

Introduction.
1. When we stand before the just God we will face the facts . . .
   (a) Not what we believe to be right . . .
   (b) Not according to our interpretation . . .
   (c) Not what we are sincere about . . .
2. Then it will be Christ or chaos . . . All hinges upon our relationship to Christ . . .
3. Four groups will be there . . .
   (a) Those condemned . . .
   (b) Those who almost get into Heaven . . .
   (c) Those whose works shall be destroyed, yet they are saved . . .
   (d) Those who are saved *wholly* . . .

I. THOSE CONDEMNED—unbelief
1. Unbelief is the basic sin of all men . . .
2. John 3:15-18 . . .
3. I John 5:1, 10-12 . . .
4. Rom. 1:16 . . .
5. Rev. 20:12-15 . . .
6. Those who spurn the new birth . . .

II. THOSE ALMOST SAVED
1. The rich young ruler—Matt. 19:16-22 . . .
2. The scribes—Mark 12:28-34 . . .
3. King Agrippa—Acts 26:24-28 . . .
4. Felix (Governor)—Acts 24:24, 25 . . .

III. THOSE EMPTY-HANDED—but saved
1. I Cor. 3:11-15—awarded according to our Christian works, witnessing for Christ . . .
2. Salvation is in Christ alone—not works . . . Rom. 3:20-28 . . . Rom. 5:1 . . .
3. Works should be the evidence of our faith . . . James 2:18 . . .
4. Must I go on empty handed (read words to song) . . .

IV. THOSE FAITHFUL CHRISTIANS WHO RECEIVE THE REWARD—I Cor. 3:14
1. Those who are saved by the blood of Christ, and labor for the glory of Christ . . .
2. Those who shall hear—"Well done"—Matt. 25:23 . . .
3. I Peter 5:4 . . .
4. I Tim. 4:7, 8 . . .
5. These receive the incorruptible crown . . . Paul says (I Cor. 9:25-27)—men strive for mastery in worldly things—we for a spiritual crown . . .

Conclusion.
1. We should walk after the Spirit—Rom. 8:1 . . .
2. We should pay the price . . . The reward is worth more than the price . . .
When YOU face the facts before a just God—WHAT THEN?

# HANDS THAT SPEAK
## JOHN 20:19-22

Introduction.  Illustration (interpretation of the painting), "Praying Hands"
—These hands speak the message of sacrifice . . . *(Christ and the Fine Arts,*
page 668)

LET US LOOK AT ANOTHER PAIR OF HANDS—THE HANDS
OF JESUS. Jesus showed his hands to the disciples . . .

I.  THEY WERE HANDS OF A LABORING MAN . . .
Jesus was a carpenter (Mark 6:3) . . .

II.  THEY WERE THE HANDS OF A SERVANT . . .
   1. Matt. 20:28, "Even as the Son of man came not to be ministered unto,
   but to minister . . .
   2. He washed the disciples' feet (John 13:4) . . .
   3. Phil. 2:7, "He made himself of no reputation, and took upon himself
   the form of a servant, and was made in the likeness of men" . . .

III.  THESE STRONG, CALLOUSED HANDS WERE TENDER
      HANDS . . .
   1. He took little children in his arms and blessed them (Mark 10:16) . . .
   2. He is so very tender in all his dealings with man . . .

IV.  THESE WERE HEALING HANDS . . .
Blind eyes—sick bodies—palsied limbs . . .

V.  THEY WERE SUPPORTING HANDS . . .
When Peter began to sink in the sea "Jesus stretched forth his hand,
and caught him" (Matt. 14:31) . . .

VI.  THESE WERE WOUNDED HANDS . . .
It was the nail prints that identified Him . . .

VII.  THESE ARE SPEAKING HANDS . . .
   1. They speak a message of love, of mercy, and of tender care . . .
   2. A message of sacrifice for each of us . . .

Conclusion:  As Jesus stretched forth his hand to save Peter—so are his
hands stretched forth to receive all who come to him . . .

PLACE YOUR HAND IN THE NAIL-SCARRED HAND.

# UNION WITH CHRIST
## ROM. 6:3-11

Introduction. "Union" does not always mean "unity"—but *union with* Christ is sweet unity. Our subject implies four things:

I. DYING WTH CHRIST—verses 6-8
 1. Paraphrased: "If we have shared the reality of His death" . . .
    (a) Seeing fully that sin merited death—He died because of sin . . .
    (b) Realizing that there can be no salvation apart from death and the shedding of blood . . .
    (c) Jesus saw the need and submitted to death on the cross . . .
 2. Death is the cessation of the former life . . .
    (a) Physical death is not the end, but the activities of the flesh cease . . .
    (b) Dying with Christ is the cessation of the former life . . .
    (1) No longer under bondage of sin . . . (2) No longer under condemnation of sin . . . (3) No longer under the guilt of sin . . . (4) Former attitudes are passed away . . .
    (c) A new concept of God . . .
    (d) A new view of worldly activities . . .
    (e) New hope . . .

II. BURIED WITH CHRIST
 1. His burial was a passageway to a more glorious life . . .
 2. We take part in His burial by putting away the former life . . .
 3. We are united with Christ . . . (a) He bore our sins in His own body—then we bear them no more . . . (b) He was made to be sin for us—and He died unto sin . . . (c) His relation to sin becomes ours . . .

III. RISING WITH CHRIST—verses 9-11
 1. In trusting Christ and His atonement we die to sin and bury the old man with Christ . . .
 2. In depending completely upon Him for salvation, we arise "New creatures in Christ Jesus" . . .
    (a) This is what Jesus meant when He said to Nicodemus, "Ye must be born again" . . .
    (b) Starting anew—this time without sin . . .
 3. Dead to sin, buried with Christ, rising to walk in newness of life . . . At this point, one is a babe in Christ . . . (1) Not yet strong . . . (2) Will have to learn to walk and talk . . . (3) He will nurture and teach . . . Pictured in baptism.

IV. WALKING WITH CHRIST
 1. If we walk with Him there must be agreement . . . Amos 3:3.
 2. To walk with another one must have faith in his companion . . . II Cor. 5:7 . . .
 3. When we walk with Christ Jesus there is no fear nor anxiety . . . (a) He will give strength for every task . . . (b) Wisdom for every decision . . . (c) Faith with every temptation . . .
 4. He will provide for every necessity . . .

Conclusion. Do you live with Christ? Are you united with Him, a new creature, living with assurance and hope? . . .
THE GIFT OF GOD IS ETERNAL LIFE—WILL YOU RECEIVE THIS GIFT??

# A PASSION FOR LOST SOULS
## ROM. 9:1-3; 10:1-4

Introduction.

These passages constitute one of the most remarkable utterances that ever fell from the lips of man—only three other statements comparable to it in the whole Word of God. (a) Moses' great prayer for the forgiveness of Israel—Ex. 32:29-33 . . . (b) Jonah when asked to be drowned to save those with whom he sailed—Jonah 1:12 . . . (c) The Lord Jesus as He faced the cross —John 12:23-28 . . . Again, on the cross—"Father, forgive them" . . .

Here is Paul's prayer, and the expression of his passion for the lost. Note what he actually says . . . (1) That he has a "great heaviness" . . . Burning compassion . . . (2) Also "unceasing sorrow in my heart" . . . A heart burdened for the lost . . . (3) "I could wish myself accursed from Christ"—I would give up my salvation, if it could save thee" . . .

What is the lesson? The message of this amazing statement? What does it teach us? THESE THREE THINGS:

I. ALL OF US OUGHT TO HAVE A GREATER CONCERN FOR THE SALVATION OF THE LOST
1. Salvation is man's greatest need . . .
2. Our greatest service and highest privilege . . .
3. The most neglected obligation of all Christians . . .
4. Often the least of our cares . . .
5. Compare Paul's concern with ours . . .
6. Jesus said, "As my Father hath sent me, even so send I you" . . .

II. THIS CONCERN OUGHT TO BE DIRECTED PARTICULARLY TOWARD OUR OWN LOVED ONES ACCORDING TO THE FLESH
1. They are our own, God given loved ones . . .
2. We owe them supreme concern and supreme prayer and effort . . .
3. No service we may render others can excuse our failures to win our own . . .
4. If we give them our best, we will not fail to win them . . .

III. THIS CONCERN FOR THE SALVATION OF MEN OUGHT TO BECOME THE CHIEF DESIRE OF OUR LIVES—Rom. 10:1-2
1. Because they are LOST . . .
2. Because they do not know God's righteousness . . .
3. Because man's sincere beliefs and God's righteousness may differ—Prov. 14:12 . . .
4. This concern will grow upon us if we will do something about it—Christianity is contagious . . . (a) Prayers . . . (b) Letters . . . (c) Personal witnessing and appeals . . .
5. When we are concerned, God will make our lives count for good things . .
6. God will not fail in winning men . . .

Conclusion.
1. Without Christ you are LOST—WILL YOU ACCEPT HIM??
2. Will you surrender your life in service??
3. Should you, under God, rededicate your life to HIM??

41

# THE CROSS
## I COR. 1:17-25

Introduction. Let us think of the cross of Christ, and the Christ of the cross . . .

I. THE MEANING OF THE CROSS
1. It is synonymous with *suffering* . . .
   (a) Christ was subjected to ridicule . . .
   (b) Was scorned by those who should have befriended Him . . .
   (c) Subjected to much anguish and suffering . . .
2. The cross meant *death* . . .
   (a) Death because of evil—SIN! . . .
   (b) The death of Christ because of our sins . . .
   (c) The shedding of innocent blood to blot out our iniquities . . .
       "Without the shedding of blood, there is no remission of sins" . . .
   (d) A substitutionary death—HE DIED FOR US . . .
3. The cross is a symbol of sacrifice . . .
   (a) As the lamb of the Old Testament was accepted as a sacrifice for the sins of the people . . .
   (b) Christ became the Lamb of God, sacrificed to redeem man . . .

II. THE MAN OF THE CROSS
1. No ordinary man—but the Son of God . . .
2. He was both God and man . . .
3. He was divine, therefore had power on earth . . . (a) To perform miracles . . . (b) To forgive sins . . .
4. He was human, therefore subject to suffering and pain . . .
5. He was the Son of God, therefore acceptable as our sacrifice for sin . . .
6. He loved us, and gave himself for us . . .
7. He could not be destroyed by crucifixion . . .
   (a) He came forth from the grave . . .
   (b) He is not dead, but alive evermore . . .
8. He is present now, calling to all who have not experienced the saving grace of God . . .
   (a) "And I, if I be lifted up, will draw . . . " . . .
   (b) "Come unto me, all ye . . . " . . .

III. THE MESSAGE OF THE CROSS—SALVATION
1. Paul said (I Cor. 2:2) . . . (a) This is the message of salvation . . . (b) It is the gospel—the atoning death . . .
2. Again Paul says (verses 17, 18) . . .
3. Verse 21 . . .

Conclusion.
1. As Christ prayed from the cross, "Father, forgive them," He was praying for YOU . . . Without Him you are doomed, eternally . . .
2. When He died on the cross—He died for YOU . . . "Without the shedding of blood"—He shed His blood . . .
3. "As many as received Him, to them gave He power to become the sons of God" . . .

WILL YOU RECEIVE HIM—*NOW??*

# PURCHASED FOR A PURPOSE
## I COR. 6:19, 20

Introduction. Paul, in this letter to the Corinthians, uses some very pointed language in an effort to make the people see that they were not the Christians they should be—verses 9-11. He deals with the facts that the Corinthians were indulging in, and giving pre-eminence to the desires and lusts of the flesh . . .

I. WE ARE A PURCHASED POSSESSION
1. The body is the Temple of the Holy Spirit . . . God created man to enjoy the vast riches of the universe—not to destroy them . . .
2. We are not our own . . .
   (a) The slave-negro could understand . . .
   (b) A purchased possession should benefit the purchaser . . . A man does not buy a horse simply because the horse needs a home . . .
3. "Bought with a price" . . .
   (a) A price which no man could possibly pay . . .
   (b) A price which could not be estimated in human equivalent . . . The nearest is the price of our national freedom . . .
   (c) "The precious blood of Christ"—Matt. 20:28 . . . Gal. 3:13 . . . I Peter 1:19 . . .
4. The body is the property of Christ—it is for the Lord . . .
   (a) Not ours—we are trustees . . .
   (b) We are to use it wisely . . .
   (c) Develop it and enjoy the God-given privileges . . .

II. WE ARE PURCHASED FOR A PURPOSE—TO GLORIFY GOD
1. The Heavens declare the glory of God . . .
2. The angels sing of His glory . . .
3. Man is purchased to glorify God . . .
4. Glorify God in your body and spirit . . . This includes all of man—*flesh, intellect, powers* . . .
5. By a visit to the cross . . . Taking Jesus as partner in life . . .
6. Loyalty . . .
   (a) To his church—no substitute . . .
   (b) Of talents . . .
   (c) To his Word . . .
7. In stewardship . . .
   (a) Of time—use it wisely . . .
   (b) Of talents . . .
   (c) Of possessions—they are His already . . .
8. Obedience and submission to the will of God . . .
   Nothing hurts more than direct disobedience . . .

Conclusion. Remember! God will allow you to do as you please. Even to your sorrow and destruction—you are the loser, not God . . .
He wants you to do His will, and thereby receive blessings for yourself and glory to God.

43

# CHRIST, OUR DELIVERER
## II COR. 1:9, 10

Introduction.
1. All men must be delivered!—all are born in sin, and under sin . . .
   (a) Ps. 51:5 . . . (b) Rom. 3:9, 10 . . .
2. Christ alone is able to deliver us . . . (a) Acts 4:12 . . . (b) Text, II Cor.
   1:9, 10 . . .

I. CHRIST DELIVERS US FROM THE PENALTY OF SIN BY THE
   SACRIFICE OF HIMSELF
   1. Col. 1:13 . . .
   2. Accomplished through His blood—Eph. 1:7 . . .
   3. Voluntary sacrifice . . .
      (a) Heb. 9:26 . . . Literal translation—"Now, once for all, at the com-
          pletion of the ages, he has been manifested for a removal of sin by
          the sacrifice of Himself." . . .
      (b) Mark 10:45 . . .
   4. A thorough cleansing—(a) I Peter 2:24 . . . (b) I John 1:7 . . .
   5. John 3:16 . . .
   6. John 3:26 . . .
   7. Heb. 10:10-12 . . .

II. CHRIST DELIVERS US FROM THE POWER OF SIN BY HIS
   1. Heb. 7:25 . . .                                    DAILY CARE
   2. II Peter 2:9 . . .
   3. Ps. 46:1 . . .
   4. He will never put more on us than we can bear . . .
   5. As a shepherd cares for his sheep . . .
   6. "Cast all your care upon Him . . . "—I Peter 5:7 . . .
   7. Our advocate—I John 2:1 . . .

III. AT HIS SECOND COMING, WHICH WLL BE PERSONAL AND
    BODILY, CHRIST WILL DELIVER US FROM THE PRESENCE OF
    1. John 14:3 . . .                                    SIN
    2. Jesus will return as He went away . . . (a) Bodily . . . (b) In the
       clouds . . .
    3. The dead in Christ shall be raised at the sound of the last trump . . .
    4. The living Christians will be transformed . . .
    5. We shall all be caught up together with the Lord, in the air—I Thess.
       4:13-17 . . .
    6. We shall be like Him—I John 3:2, 3 . . . (a) Sinless . . . (b) Glori-
       fied . . .

Conclusion. To summarize:
1. You are delivered from the guilt and penalty of sin because Jesus came
   and died as your substitute . . .
2. You are delivered from the power of sin (the daily attempts of Satan
   to overthrow you) because Jesus lives and intercedes . . .
3. You will be delivered from the presence of sins when Jesus comes
   again . . . To receive His own . . .

Have YOU been delivered from sin through believing on, and trusting
Jesus—in faith? . . .
Are YOU being delivered daily through His presence and power? . . .
Are YOU ready to be delivered unto the Father? . . .

# THE MOTIVATING POWER IN CHRISTIANITY
## II COR. 5:14

Introduction. The motivating power in almost everything is LOVE . . .

1. The love of freedom brought our forefathers to suffer the hardships in a new country . . .
2. Love builds and maintains homes . . .
3. The love of money, or power, or position has destroyed many a man . . .
4. The love for praise (of man) has corrupted many lives . . . .
5. The love of a mother for her child causes her to care for the babe, day and night . . . Never tiring, nor complaining . . .
6. None can compare with the love of God . . . (a) For us . . . (b) In us . . . (c) Through us . . .

I. THE MOTIVATING POWER THAT PROMPTED THE PROVISION FOR OUR REDEMPTION WAS THE *LOVE* OF GOD—I John 4:10
   1. It was God's love that brought Him looking for Adam in the Garden . . .
   2. His love provided the covering for Adam's nakedness . . .
   3. God's love provided for, and preserved mankind through Noah . . . (a) God's patience with man was at an end . . . (b) He destroyed every thing, yet preserved enough to replenish the earth . . .
   4. God's love sent Moses to lead Israel out of Egypt . . .
   5. God's love motivated His patience with the children in the wilderness . . .
   6. God's love sent Jesus—John 3:16 . . . (a) To fulfill all Scripture . . . (b) To be the propitiation for sin . . . (c) To complete and offer salvation . . .

II. THE MOTIVATING POWER THAT COMPLETED REDEMPTION WAS THE *LOVE* OF CHRIST—Rev. 1:5; Eph. 5:2
   1. We see this love at the grave of Lazarus . . . At the gate of Nain . . . At the well of Samaria . . . As He wept over Jerusalem . . .
   2. As He prayed for us—John 17 . . .
   3. In Gethsemane . . .
   4. Reconciliation at Calvary . . .
   5. Forgiveness and daily leadership . . .
   6. The consummation of salvation in eternity . . . (a) John 14:1-4 . . . (b) Coming for us . . . (c) Receiving us . . .

III. THE MOTIVATING POWER IN CHRISTIAN LIVING IS OUR *LOVE FOR* CHRIST—Eph. 3:17-19
   1. "*Christ* in you the hope of glory" — Col. 1:27 . . .
   2. "If you love me, keep my commandments"—John 14:15 . . . (a) Love your neighbors—friends and enemies alike . . . (b) Witness for Him . . . (c) Live consistent Christian lives . . .
   3. Love for Christ makes us work together for the glory of God . . .

Conclusion. Our prayer for each one—Eph. 3:17-19.

DO YOU HAVE THIS LOVE??

# SEPARATED FOR GOD
## II COR. 6:14-18

Introduction.  Regeneration is a form of segregation—Christians are in the world, but not a part of the world . . .
   1. John 17:12-16 . . .
   2. Rom. 12:1, 2 . . .
The words of our text are words of admonition to Christians and an invitation to non-Christians . . .

I.  CHRISTIANS OUGHT TO BE A SEPARATED PEOPLE
   1. Verse 14a—Christians should not be bound to non-Christians . . .
      (a) In marriage . . .
      (b) In organizations . . .
      (c) In business . . .
      (d) Even in religious endeavor . . .
   2. Verses 14-16—In these verses are listed five synonymous questions which, when answered, will show why Christians ought to be a separated people . . .
   3. "Ye are the temple of the living God"—verse 16b . . .
      (a) I Cor. 3:16, 17 . . .
      (b) I Cor. 6:19, 20 . . .

II.  THERE IS GREAT DANGER IN INTEGRATION (not separated)
   1. Evil usually contaminates good . . .
      (a) Bad onion in a basket . . .
      (b) A drop of poison in a glass of water . . .
      (c) Oil mixed with water destroys the usefulness of both . . .
   2. Illustrated by the union of Christian and Communist . . .

III.  COMMAND CONCERNING SEPARATION—verse 17
   1. "Come out from among them, and be ye separate" . . .
   2. Not drive them away from . . .
      (a) Separate yourselves . . .
      (b) Although thrown together live separated lives . . .
          Even in marriage Christians should live separate lives . . . This vital issue should be carefully considered before marriage . . .
   3. Not force others to meet your standards, but you are to meet God's standards . . .
      (a) You must account only for you . . .
      (b) Ill.—the incident at High Point . . .

IV.  INCENTIVE AND ENCOURAGEMENT FOR SEPARATION—
   1. A father loves his children . . .                    verse 18 . . .
   2. He educates them . . .
      (a) By teaching them . . .
      (b) By providing for further education . . .
   3. He guards them . . .
   4. He provides for them . . .
Conclusion.  "Come out from among them"—and claim the promises of God.

# PERSONAL INVENTORY
## II COR. 13:5-11

Introduction. In this passage we see two exhortations (verse 5, 11): each suggests that we examine ourselves ...

1. "I" is the most important letter in the alphabet ...
   (a) It is the person you see in the mirror ...
   (b) The person responsible for your every action ...
2. Something else we should see about "I"—It is in the center of "sin," "pride," and "Saviour" ...

## I. 'I" IS THE CENTER OF SIN

1. Sin is transgression of God's law ...
2. That which defiles the man—Mark 7:20-23 ..
3. Sin separates from God—Isa. 59:2 ...
4. Sin hinders prayer and power—Ps. 66:18 ...
5. Sin excludes from Heaven—I Cor. 6:9-11 ...
6. Sin is forgiveable—Eph. 1:7 ...
   The blood of Christ takes "I" out of sin ...

## II. "I" IS THE CENTER OF PRIDE—Luke 18:11-14

1. The Pharisee's greatest sin was pride—"I" ...
2. Prov. 16:18 ...
3. Pharaoh's pride destroyed him—Ex. 5:2 ...
4. Naaman's pride almost cost him his life—II Kings 5:1-11 ...
5. Pride destroys humility and builds a wall between you and God ...

## III. "I" IS THE CENTER OF SAVIOUR

1. John 14:15-20 ...
2. Rom. 8:1 ...
3. Enter by faith—Eph. 3:17 ...
4. In Christ you are a new creature—Gal. 2:20 ...
5. To be in Christ is to know the joy of salvation ...
6. In Him is our faith and hope ...
7. In Him is our comfort and strength ...
8. Acts 17:28 ...

Conclusion. He is our eternal security.

ARE YOU *IN* HIM?

# THE OBJECT OF GOD'S LOVE
## EPH. 2:1-9 — TEXT, II COR. 12:14

Introduction. What does God want of man? The object of God's love is, NOT YOURS BUT *YOU* . . .

1. Not riches—They are His . . .
2. Not the world—He made it . . .
3. Not power—He is power . . .

*GOD WANTS YOU* . . .

I. NOT TO MAKE YOU A SLAVE TO A SET OF RELIGIOUS RULES
1. Some are slaves to their religion . . .
   (a) Living in fear and superstition . . .
   (b) Abusing their bodies in appeasement . . .
2. Christianity is not a long-faced religion that prevents all enjoyment . . . Instead, it:
   (a) Produces joy unspeakable—John 16:20 . . .
   (b) Puts happiness in our heart and a smile on our faces . . .
3. Christianity is freedom rather than enslavement . . .

II. THAT HE MIGHT BRING YOU TO CHRIST
1. The law was given to this end—Gal. 3:24 . . .
2. The need of salvation must be considered . . .
   (a) Rom 3:23 . . .
   (b) Rom. 3:10 . . .
   (c) Isa. 53:6 . . .
3. The means of salvation has been provided . . .
   (a) Rom. 5:8 . . .
   (b) Eph. 2:8, 9 . . .
   (c) I Peter 2:24 . . .

III. THAT HE MIGHT LEAD YOU IN A GLORIOUSLY HAPPY LIFE
   —A full and complete life . . . And prepare you for the life to come . . .

Conclusion. Five things to consider . . .

1. That God wants you . . .
2. That your greatest need is salvation . . .
3. That salvation is complete in Christ . .
4. That you are invited to receive Him by faith . . .
5. That you may live a happy, victorious life—BEGINNING NOW . . .

# THREE WAYS TO LOOK AT THE ATONEMENT
## PHIL. 2:5-8

Introduction.   Many words are used in the Scripture denoting the atonement
—several theories . . .

- (a)  Accident theory . . .
- (b)  Martyr . . .
- (c)  Moral influence . . .
- (d)  Love of God . . .
- (e)  Predetermined . . .
- (f)  Voluntary . . .
- (g)  Vicarious . . .
- (h)  Sacrificial . . .
- (i)  Expiatory . . .
- (j)  Propitiatory . . .
- (k)  Redemptive . . .
- (l)  Substitutionary . . .

We are not concerned about any of these in particular . . . We consider three
ways to look at the atonement—all of which are correct . . .

I.   THE WORLD SENT JESUS TO THE CROSS—I Cor. 2:7, 8

1. His contemporaries—the religious leaders . . .
2. The men of the street—the general public . . .
3. Formalism . . .
4. Politics . . .
5. Society . . .
6. Sin—our sin . . .

II.   JESUS SENT HIMSELF TO THE CROSS—I Peter 2:24

1. Jesus faced the cross in all His ministry . . .
2. Many times He referred to the sacrifice of His life . . .

III.   GOD SENT JESUS TO THE CROSS—Isa. 53:6

1. This was the plan and prophecy from the beginning . . .
2. The only means of satisfying divine justice . . . Through the cross
   justice and mercy are brought together . . .

Conclusion.   God was in Christ reconciling the world to Himself . . .

# CONSIDER CHRIST
## HEB. 3:1-4; 12:3

Introduction.
1. When there is a problem—consider Christ.
2. When troubled or burdened . . . consider Christ.
3. When anxious—consider Christ.
4. Consider Christ—Let Him govern your life.

I. THE MAN
1. He was kind—"Suffer little children . . . " (Mark 10:13, 14) . . .
2. He was sympathetic . . .
   (a) Wept at the grave of Lazarus . . .
   (b) Wept over Jerusalem . . .
   (c) Sympathetic with all who were burdened . . .
3. He was compassionate . . .
   (a) When the leper came to Him (Mark 1:41) . . .
   (b) He looked at the multitudes (Mark 6:34) . . .
   (c) Blind cried for mercy (Matt. 20:34) . . .
   (d) At the gate of Nain( Luke 7:11-15) . . .
   (e) As a man, Jesus suffered with others—How much more as the Saviour? . . .
4. He was perfect . . .

II. THE TEACHER
1. Recognized in youth—in the Temple . . .
2. In manhood (John 3:2) . . .
3. In the synagogue (Mark 6:2-6) . . .
4. He taught with authority . . .
   His work *was* and *is* final . . .

III. THE SAVIOUR
1. He was sent from God . . .
2. Sent for a purpose (John 3:17; Luke 19:10) . . .
3. Was submissive to God's will and purpose (John 6:38) . . .
4. He accomplished the work he was sent to do (John 17:1-4 and John 19:30) . . .
5. He is the only Saviour (Acts 4:12) . . .

IV. THE HIGH PRIEST
1. He knows our needs (Heb. 2:17 and 4:15) . . .
2. He is at God's right hand (Heb. 10:12) . . .
3. Our High Priest eternally . . . (Heb 7:25) . . .

Conclusion. CONSIDER CHRIST . . .
1. As a man He set the perfect example . . .
2. As a teacher, He set forth the perfect plan for salvation and life . . .
3. As the Saviour, He provides flawless redemption . . .
4. As our High Priest, He observes and provides our every need . . .

WON'T YOU CONSIDER CHRIST?

# THE VOICE OUT OF THE DEEP
## LUKE 16:19-31

Introduction. Text, v. 24—This voice expresses a universal need—a universal appeal . . . Sooner or later every person will call upon God for mercy. Unfortunately, many, like Dives, will call too late . . .

This message echoes Isaiah's warning. He said, Isaiah 56:6, 7 . . .
Let us note:

I. HE CRIED FOR MERCY. v. 24
   The universal need . . .
   1. Numerous times in Psalms, the plea, "Have mercy on us" . . .
   2. Two blind men followed Jesus crying, "Have mercy on me" . . .
   3. The woman whose daughter was vexed with a devil cried, "Have mercy on me" . . .
   4. The Publican cried, "Be merciful to me, a sinner" . . .
   5. Each of these cried because they realized there was no other source of help . . .
      They did not ask for justice—but mercy . . .
   6. Let us get back to Dives . . .
      (a) What did he actually deserve from God? . . .
      (b) Had left God out of his whole life . . . had taken things in his own hands . . .
          He had his reward . . .
      (c) Why did he not mention who he was? . . .
          He was only an individual—God is no respecter of persons . . .
      (d) Why did he not want justice . . .
          He was now experiencing justice . . .

II. HE CRIED FOR PERSONAL HELP. v. 24

III. HE PLEADED FOR THE SALVATION OF OTHERS. v. 27-28 . . .
   1. Those in torment do not want company . . .
   2. Not enough *good things* in life to make eternity without God worthwhile . . .

IV. GOD'S ANSWER . . .
   1. V. 24. You sinned away your opportunity—had your chance . . .
   2. V. 26. Too late now . . .
   3. V. 29-31. Everyone has equal opportunity . . . Man is completely without excuse (Rom. 1:20 and 2:1) . . .

Conclusion. God's mercy is available—After life is over, it is too late.

51

# THE GRACE OF GOD

Introduction.                   I COR. 15:10, 11

1. "Grace"—What is grace? . . . Unmerited favor—the redemption plan of God in saving sinners and sustaining them in the right relationship . . .
2. Grace is described as,
   (a) Great (Acts 4:33) . . .
   (b) Sovereign (Rom. 5:21) . . .
   (c) Rich (Eph. 1:7) . . .
   (d) Exceeding (II Cor. 9:14) . . .
   (e) Manifold (I Peter 4:10) . . .
   (f) All-sufficient (II Cor. 12:9) . . .
   (g) Abundant (Rom. 5:17) . . .
   (h) Glorious (Eph. 1:6) . . .
3. It is the source of,
   (a) Election (Rom. 11:15) . . .
   (b) The call of God (Gal. 1:15) . . .
   (c) Justification (Rom. 3:24) . . .
   (d) Faith (Acts 18:27) . . .
   (e) Forgiveness (Eph. 1:7-9) . . .
   (f) Salvation (Eph. 2:5-9) . . .
   (g) Consolation (II Thess. 2:16) . . .
   (h) Hope . . .
4. It is specifically given,
   (a) To Ministers (Rom. 12:6) . . .
   (b) To the humble (James 4:6) . . .
   (c) To those who walk uprightly (Ps. 84:11) . . .
5. Paul says it was the grace of God that made him what he was! . . .

Let us note what this grace does for us:

I. GOD'S GRACE FOUND US . . .
   Man does not seek God—God seeks man (Rom. 3:10-11) . . .
   1. Think of Moses . . .
   2. Matthew . . .
   3. Zacchaeus . . .
   4. Paul . . .
   5. Personally applied—Where did God find *me?* . . .

II. GOD'S GRACE SAVED US . . .
   1. Eph. 2:8-9 . . .
   2. Rom. 3:21-26 . . .
      (a) Man wholly without merit—justified freely by His grace . . .
      (b) The imputed righteousness of Christ Jesus . . .
      (c) Paul was wholly conscious of this when he prayed for Israel (Rom. 10:1-4) . . .

III. GOD'S GRACE FITS US FOR OUR TASK . . . EMPOWERS . . .
   1. Text . . .
   2. Gal. 1:15-16 . . .
   3. Rom. 12:6-8 . . .
   4. God's grace is sufficient (II Cor. 12:9) . . .
   5. One other thing, we need to be fitted for—Support the Kingdom work (II Cor. 8:7-8) . . .

Conclusion. We are exhorted to "Grow in grace and in the knowledge of our Lord and Saviour, Jesus Christ."

# A PUZZLED CHRIST
## MARK 6:1-6

Introduction. Here is an incident where the Word of God was preached—the Spirit of God was felt—the Power of God was known. Yet, the Lord himself was powerless to reach these people. Why? Because of their unbelief . . . Jesus was puzzled—He had poured out His heart to no avail . . .

This may very well be a picture of any congregation today— Seeing but not seeing, hearing but not hearing, experiencing the presence of God but refusing to believe and respond . . .

Let us note:

I. UNBELIEF . . .
  1. They were astonished at His teachings, yet refused to believe, v. 2 . . .
  2. They knew all about Him, yet refused to believe, v. 3 . . .
  3. They knew about His mighty works, yet refused to believe . . .

II. CAUSES OF UNBELIEF . . .
  1. The natural depravity of man . . .
     The first sin was unbelief . . .
  2. Spiritual blindness . . .
  3. The love of sin . . .
  4. Egotism and pride . . .
  5. Self-righteousness . . .
  6. Satan himself is a great preacher of unbelief . . .
     Unbelief is the result of listening to Satan . . .

III. EFFECTS, OR RESULTS OF UNBELIEF . . .
  1. Unbelief is an insult to God . . .
  2. It refutes all the promises of God's Word . . .
     The promises of blessings and of judgment . . .
  3. It cancels out the work of Christ . . .
     No mighty work because of their unbelief . . .
  4. Unbelief makes you a sinner—and keeps you a sinner because it keeps you from accepting Christ . . .
  5. It places one under sentence of condemnation . . . "Condemned already . . . "
  6. It renders useless the atonement of Christ . . .
     The unbeliever refuses the feast of God and the Water of life . . .
  7. Unbelief is keeping you from surrendereing your whole life to Christ . . .
  8. Unbelief keeps you from being loyal to Christ and His church . . .
  9. Unbelief will rob you of God's blessings . . .

Conclusion. Is it any wonder that the Lord Jesus was puzzled—He poured out His soul, gave His all—yet they refused to believe . . .
### IS HE PUZZLED TODAY???
  1. He gave His life for your salvation . . .
  2. The Holy Spirit for your conviction . . .
  3. His providential blessings for your welfare . . .
  4. His Word for your edification . . .
  5. His promise for your hope . . .

YET SOME REFUSE TO BELIEVE! FAITH IS THE ONLY REMEDY FOR UNBELIEF . . .

# WHEN WE STAND BEFORE GOD
## REV. 20:11-15

Introduction.  At the end of this age several things must come to pass . . .
1. Jesus will return to gather His own . . .
   (a) As He left (Acts 1:11)—as He promised (John 14:3) . . .
   (b) This is the first resurrection, v. 5-6 . . .
   I Thess. 4:15-17 . . .
2. The manifestation of works—I Cor. 3:13-15 . . .
3. The Tribulation—Millennium, v. 4-6 . . .
4. The Final Judgment—WE STAND BEFORE GOD . . .
   (a) This is the time when "every knee shall bow, and every tongue shall confess that Jesus Christ is Lord . . . "
   (b) This is the "Great Day," the Day of the Lord . . .

I.  WE SHALL STAND BEFORE *GOD* . . .
1. God, whose face no man can see and live . . .
2. God, whose glory was revealed to Isaiah . . . Isa. 6:1-8 . . .
3. God, Who is omniscient and omnipotent . . .
4. God, whose WORD is the final authority . . . Interpretations and opinions will not count here . . .
5. God, who is altogether holy and righteous . . .
6. God, who created the earth—and also shall destroy it . . .

II.  *WE* SHALL STAND BEFORE GOD . . .
1. The destiny of Christians was sealed at Calvary . . .
   But they will be there, v. 4 . . .
2. Every person will be there, v. 12-13 . . .
3. We will be there . . .

III.  WE SHALL *STAND* BEFORE GOD . . .
1. Christians shall hear, "Come, ye blessed of my Father . . . " (Matt. 25:34) . . .
2. All others shall hear,
   (a) "I never knew, depart from me, ye that work iniquity." (Matt. 7:23) . . .
   (b) "Depart from me, ye cursed, into everlasting fire, prepared for the devil and his angels" . . .
3. These are cast into Hell, v. 14-15 . . .

Conclusion:

There will be no mercy here—only judgment . . .
1. Pronunciation of the sentence of death . . .
2. Separation—from God, loved ones, friends . . .
3. *THIS IS WHY JESUS GAVE HIS ALL*—that you may avoid the second death . . .